GOVERNMENT PROCEDURES AND OPERATIONS

FEDERAL REGULATIONS

COST ESTIMATION, RULEMAKING ACTIVITY, AND COST-BENEFIT ISSUES

GOVERNMENT PROCEDURES AND OPERATIONS

Additional books in this series can be found on Nova's website under the Series tab.

Additional e-books in this series can be found on Nova's website under the eBooks tab.

GOVERNMENT PROCEDURES AND OPERATIONS

FEDERAL REGULATIONS

COST ESTIMATION, RULEMAKING ACTIVITY, AND COST-BENEFIT ISSUES

JAMIE P. DAVIDSON
EDITOR

NOVINKA

New York

NOTICE TO THE READER

Additional color graphics may be available in the e-book version of this book.

Library of Congress Cataloging-in-Publication Data

ISBN: 978-1-63485-312-5

Published by Nova Science Publishers, Inc. † New York

CONTENTS

PREFACE

Federal agencies issue thousands of regulations each year under delegated authority from Congress. Over the past 70 years, Congress and various Presidents have created a set of procedures agencies must follow to issue these regulations, some of which contain requirements for the calculation and consideration of costs, benefits, and other economic effects of regulations. In recent years, many Members of Congress have expressed an interest in various regulatory reform efforts that would change the current set of rulemaking requirements, including requirements to estimate costs and benefits of regulations. As part of this debate, it has become common for supporters of regulatory reform to comment on the total cost of federal regulation. This book discusses methods of estimating the total cost of federal regulations. Furthermore, the book serves to inform the congressional debate over rulemaking by analyzing different ways to measure federal rulemaking activity; describes the existing requirements for cost-benefit and other types of analysis in the federal rulemaking process; and discusses options for changing the current set of analytical requirements.

In: Federal Regulations
Editor: Jamie P. Davidson

ISBN: 978-1-63485-312-5

Chapter 1

METHODS OF ESTIMATING THE TOTAL COST OF FEDERAL REGULATIONS*

Maeve P. Carey

SUMMARY

Federal agencies issue thousands of regulations each year under delegated authority from Congress. Over the past 70 years, Congress and various Presidents have created a set of procedures agencies must follow to issue these regulations, some of which contain requirements for the calculation and consideration of costs, benefits, and other economic effects of regulations. In recent years, many Members of Congress have expressed an interest in various regulatory reform efforts that would change the current set of rulemaking requirements, including requirements to estimate costs and benefits of regulations. As part of this debate, it has become common for supporters of regulatory reform to comment on the total cost of federal regulation.

Estimating the total cost of regulations is inherently difficult. Current estimates of the cost of regulation should be viewed with a great deal of caution.

Scholars and governmental entities estimating the total cost of regulation use one of two methods, which are referred to as the "bottom-up" and the "top-down" approach. The bottom-up approach aggregates

* This is an edited, reformatted and augmented version of a Congressional Research Service publication R44348, prepared for Members and Committees of Congress, dated January 21, 2016.

individual cost and benefit estimates produced by agencies, arriving at a government-wide total. In 2014, the annual report to Congress from the Office of Management and Budget estimated the total cost of federal regulations to range between $68.5 and $101.8 billion and the total benefits to be between $261.7 billion and $1,042.1 billion. The top-down approach estimates the total cost of regulation by looking at the relationship of certain macroeconomic factors, including the size of a country's economy and a proxy measure of how much regulation the country has. This method estimates the economic effect that a hypothetical change in the amount of regulation in the United States might have, considering that economic effect to represent the cost of regulation. One frequently cited study estimated the total cost of regulation in 2014 to be $2.028 trillion, $1.439 trillion of which was calculated using this top-down approach.

Each approach has inherent advantages and disadvantages. The bottom-up approach relies on agency estimates of the effects of specific regulations and can also be used to estimate benefits, because agencies typically estimate both costs and benefits under current requirements so that they may be compared and evaluated against alternatives. The bottom-up approach does not, however, include estimates of costs and benefits of *all* rules, nor does it include costs and benefits of regulations that are not monetized—meaning that the bottom-up approach is likely an underestimate of the total cost of regulation. Furthermore, the individual estimates produced by agencies and used in the bottom-up approach may not always be accurate.

The top-down approach can be used to estimate effects of rules that are not captured by the bottom-up approach—such as indirect costs and costs of rules issued by independent regulatory agencies, which are not included in the bottom-up approach—thus theoretically capturing the whole universe of regulatory costs. Its results are, however, entirely reliant upon a number of methodological challenges that are difficult, if not impossible, to overcome. The biggest challenge may be finding a valid proxy measure for regulation: proxy measures of the total amount of regulation in a country are inherently imprecise and cannot be reliably used to estimate macroeconomic outcomes. Because of this difficulty in identifying a suitable proxy measure of regulation, even if the total cost of regulation is substantial, it cannot be estimated with any precision. The top-down method is intended to measure only costs; measuring costs without also considering benefits does not provide the complete context for evaluating the appropriateness of a country's amount of regulation.

For these and other reasons, both approaches to estimating the total cost of regulation have inherent—and potentially insurmountable—flaws. The discrepancy between the two approaches and their associated estimates raises the question of the utility of using such figures in the regulatory reform debate.

ESTIMATING THE TOTAL COSTS AND BENEFITS OF FEDERAL REGULATION

Federal agencies issue thousands of regulations every year. These regulations are often the means through which various government policies and programs are implemented. Many of these regulations are administrative or routine in nature and have little or no compliance cost associated with them.[1] A number of these regulations can, however, have a substantial effect on the economy in the form of costs, benefits, and transfer payments. Over the past 70 years, Congress and various Presidents have created a set of procedures agencies must follow to issue these regulations, some of which contain requirements for the calculation and consideration of costs, benefits, and other economic effects of regulations.[2]

Federal regulations are the product of delegated legislative authority from Congress—agencies may promulgate regulations only with the authority from Congress to do so. As such, Congress has shown an interest in conducting oversight of those regulations, both on the individual level for particular regulations and also for the regulatory system as a whole. One way for Congress to conduct oversight of the regulatory system as a whole, some say, is to monitor the total cost and benefits of federal regulation. Comparing the estimated costs against the benefits would provide some insight into the potential tradeoffs of regulation.

In recent years, many Members of Congress have expressed interest in various regulatory reform efforts that would change the rulemaking process.[3] Proponents of these efforts argue that the system under which agencies currently issue federal regulations is outdated, and that federal agencies should be required to conduct more rigorous economic analysis of their regulations.[4] Opponents of these regulatory reform efforts argue that adding to federal rulemaking requirements could cause fewer regulations to be issued by federal agencies or could create delays in the issuance of federal regulations.[5] As part of this debate, it has become common for supporters of regulatory reform to comment on the total cost of federal regulation.

Estimating the total cost of regulations is inherently difficult. Current estimates of the cost of regulation should be viewed with a great deal of caution.

Scholars attempting to identify an estimate for the total cost of regulation have taken two primary approaches that lead to radically different conclusions about the total economic effect of regulation. In this report, these two approaches are referred to as the "bottom-up" and the "top-down" approaches or methods. In short, the bottom-up approach aggregates individual cost estimates produced by federal agencies. The top-down approach relies on macroeconomic modeling to find a causal relationship between larger economic factors, such as gross domestic product (GDP), and a proxy measure intended to represent the overall amount of regulation.[6]

The two approaches use entirely different methods and produce radically different results. In 2014, the most frequently cited cost estimates resulting from each of these studies ranged from $57-$87 billion (using the bottom-up method) to $2 trillion (the majority—almost $1.5 trillion— of which was arrived at using the top-down method).[7]

This report analyzes these two approaches for estimating the total cost of federal regulations. In discussing each approach, the report provides an overview of the advantages, a brief case study, and an analysis of the potential issues or inherent problems using the case study to illustrate the concepts.

The objective of this report is not to provide an estimate of the total costs and benefits of federal regulations, but rather, to inform the broader regulatory reform debate by identifying the difficulties in providing such estimates and potential problems inherent in the methods that exist.

"Bottom-Up" Method: Aggregating Existing Cost Estimates

The first approach to aggregating the total costs and benefits of federal rules is generally referred to as a "bottom-up" approach.

What Is the Bottom-Up Approach?

This method relies on estimates of costs and benefits that agencies produce during the rulemaking process, pursuant to several requirements.[8] The bottom-up approach aggregates these estimates of costs and benefits that agencies calculate in individual rulemakings, using the sum as a government-wide total. Understanding the requirements under which agencies conduct these estimates—specifically, knowing *when* agencies are required to estimate costs and benefits, and when they are not—is important for understanding the advantages and disadvantages of the bottom-up approach.

The primary requirement for most agencies to calculate estimates of costs and benefits when issuing rules is under Executive Order 12866.[9] That executive order requires covered agencies to assess costs and benefits for "economically significant" rules at the proposed and final rule stage.[10] Economically significant rules are defined in the executive order as those that may "have an annual effect on the economy of $100 million or more or adversely affect in a material way the economy, a sector of the economy, productivity, competition, jobs, the environment, public health or safety, or State, local, or tribal governments or communities."[11] The term "effect on the economy" means that a rule may be considered economically significant if it has costs *or* benefits of over $100 million.[12] Other provisions of Executive Order 12866 encourage agencies to consider costs and benefits during the rulemaking process for all rules, although those other provisions do not require a complete, detailed cost-benefit analysis for non-economically significant rules.[13] Executive Order 12866, issued by President Clinton, has remained in effect since 1993, and it was reaffirmed in 2011 by President Obama in Executive Order 13563.[14] The estimates that agencies produce under Executive Order 12866 are subject to review by the Office of Management and Budget (OMB). Specifically, agencies submit their rules and cost-benefit analyses to OMB's Office of Information and Regulatory Affairs (OIRA), the agency within OMB responsible for reviewing regulations and cost-benefit analyses. OMB has issued a number of guidance documents agencies are required to follow when estimating costs and benefits of regulations.[15]

In addition to these executive order requirements, certain statutory requirements for cost-benefit analysis, or other types of regulatory impact analysis, sometimes require agencies to calculate costs, benefits, and other economic effects of rules. The Regulatory Flexibility Act (RFA) requires regulatory impact analyses for proposed and final rules that will have a "significant economic impact on a substantial number of small entities."[16] Title II of the Unfunded Mandates Reform Act (UMRA) requires agencies to analyze and reduce costs associated with federal mandates upon state, local, and tribal governments and the private sector.[17] However, in practice, the RFA and UMRA apply to a fairly small number of rules. Finally, agencies may be required under their own authorizing statutes to calculate and/or consider the costs and benefits of their rules.

The bottom-up approach for estimating costs and benefits aggregates the estimates produced under these requirements, producing a total, government-wide figure for the costs and benefits of regulation.

Why Use the Bottom-Up Approach?

The bottom-up approach to estimating the costs and benefits of federal regulation has several potential benefits. First, this approach sums up actual estimates of costs and benefits that agencies have calculated for individual regulations, and, as described above, most of these estimates have undergone review from OMB.

Second, under the requirements discussed above, agencies estimate both costs and benefits, which allows the bottom-up approach to compare total estimated costs to total estimated benefits. Such information can be valuable for evaluation of cost-effectiveness of regulation generally (i.e., what the benefits received are for the costs invested) and it allows for calculation and evaluation of a ratio of costs to benefits.

Third, the components of the bottom-up approach to measuring costs and benefits could be validated by conducting analysis *ex post*, or after the fact, of what the costs and benefits of specific regulations actually turned out to be.[18] This could be done, for example, as part of agencies' retrospective review process, in which agencies reanalyze existing rules and may consider making amendments to those rules in light of the *ex post* analysis. Agencies do not always conduct retrospective review of their regulations, however, and a retrospective review does not necessarily include a reevaluation of the initial cost-benefit analysis to test its accuracy.[19] But some such studies have been conducted in recent years by scholars and observers of the regulatory process.[20]

Despite these and other potential advantages of using a bottom-up approach to aggregating costs and benefits, certain issues—and potential caveats—should be taken into consideration. To help illustrate some of these issues, this report first introduces a case study: the most well-known and widely cited bottom-up study of the total costs and benefits of regulation. The report then uses the case study to analyze and discuss some of the problems with a bottom-up study.

Case Study: The Annual OMB Report on the Total Costs and Benefits of Federal Rules

The most well-known bottom-up study is the report to Congress on the benefits and costs of federal rules, which OMB compiles annually.[21]

Background on the OMB Report to Congress

Since the 1990s, OMB has estimated the total costs and benefits of federal regulations pursuant to various federal requirements. The initial requirement was in Section 645 of the Treasury, Postal Service and General Government Appropriations Act, 1997,[22] which required the Director of OMB to submit a report by September 30, 1997, that provided—among other things—"estimates of the total annual costs and benefits of federal regulatory programs, including quantitative and nonquantitative measures of regulatory costs and benefits." Similar requirements were contained in other appropriations bills in subsequent years; as of 2015, the current requirement for OMB to report on the total annual costs and benefits of federal regulations is under the Regulatory Rightto-Know Act, which was enacted in 2000 as part of the Treasury and General Government Appropriations Act for FY2001.[23] That provision required OMB to submit to Congress each year, along with the President's budget,

An accounting statement and associated report containing-

1) an estimate of the total annual costs and benefits (including quantifiable and nonquantifiable effects) of Federal rules and paperwork, to the extent feasible- (A) in the aggregate; (B) by agency and agency program; and (C) by major rule;
2) an analysis of impacts of Federal regulation on State, local, and tribal government, small business, wages, and economic growth; and
3) recommendations for reform.

OMB has submitted a report to Congress each year with a total of the costs and benefits produced by federal agencies pursuant to the requirements discussed above.

Summary of 2014 OMB Report on Costs and Benefits

The 2014 report to Congress on the costs and benefits of federal regulations was published in June 15, 2015.[24] The principal findings of the 2014 report were as follows:[25]

- The estimated annual benefits of major federal regulations reviewed by OMB from October 1, 2003, to September 30, 2013, for which agencies estimated and monetized both benefits and costs, are in the aggregate between $281.0 billion and $1,119.0 billion, while the estimated annual costs are in the aggregate between $73.6 billion and $109.3 billion.[26] These ranges reflect uncertainty in the benefits and costs of each rule at the time that it was evaluated (prior to promulgation).

The OMB reports demonstrate that agencies do not provide quantified and/or monetized information for every rule. For example, below is information on how frequently agencies provided quantified and/or monetized estimates of costs and benefits:

- During FY2013, executive agencies promulgated 54 major rules, of which 30 were "transfer" rules.[27] Transfer rules usually implement federal budgetary programs as required or authorized by Congress, such as rules associated with the Medicare Program and the Federal Pell Grant Program, and are categorized differently by OMB because they cause income transfers from federally collected tax dollars to program beneficiaries—meaning they "may not impose significant regulatory costs on the private sector."[28] In all but one of the 30 transfer rules listed in the report, the issuing agencies quantified and monetized the transfer amounts.
- In 7 of the remaining 24 major rules issued in FY2013, the agencies quantified and monetized both benefits and costs. Those seven rules were estimated to result in a total of $33.2 billion to $87.4 billion in annual benefits, and $2.6 billion to $3.2 billion in annual costs.[29]
- In two of the major rules, the agency was able to quantify and monetize only benefits. For these two rules, the agencies estimated annual benefits of $500 million to $655 million.[30]
- In 11 major rules, the agencies quantified and monetized only costs, and in one case only partially. For these 11 rules, the agencies estimated total annual costs of about $1.6 billion to $2.3 billion.[31]
- In four major rules, the agencies did not quantify or monetize costs or benefits.

Quantification vs. Monetization

Quantification of costs and benefits involves identifying quantitative effects of regulations, such as identifying a number of persons or businesses likely to be affected by a rule. Monetization involves turning effects of rules specifically into dollar amounts so that they may be aggregated and compared.

In some cases, a rule's effects may be easy to quantify but difficult to monetize.

Analysis of Bottom-Up Approach to Aggregating Costs and Benefits

A bottom-up approach, such as that taken by OMB, is likely to result in an underestimate of the total cost of federal regulations. Agencies are not required to conduct a cost-benefit analysis for every rule, and the bottom-up approach can only include costs and benefits that have actually been estimated. Furthermore, estimates of costs and benefits that agencies produce are primarily intended to inform decisionmakers about an individual rule, but aggregating the information causes the context and understanding of potential uncertainties in each individual estimate to be lost. Finally, a decision must be made about how many years' worth of rules to include in the aggregated estimate of costs and benefits, but this is likely to leave out costs and benefits of rules that were issued prior to the period included.

Costs Not Estimated for Every Rule

One of the main challenges to calculating accurately the total costs and benefits of federal regulations is that agencies are not required to estimate costs and benefits for all regulations. Without an estimated cost or benefit for every rule, it is impossible to arrive at a total dollar amount for all rules—the aggregated costs and benefits will only include those rules for which a monetized estimate exists.

Independent Regulatory Agencies Are Often Not Required to Estimate Costs and Benefits

First, not all agencies are subject to cost-benefit analysis requirements. The cost-benefit analysis requirement does not apply to independent regulatory agencies, a class of agencies that were created by Congress to have various characteristics of independence from the President.[32]

Although some of the independent regulatory agencies have agency-specific instructions in statute to consider certain effects of their regulations, others are not specifically required to conduct cost-benefit analysis or monetize costs and benefits.[33] According to OMB's 2014 report on costs and benefits, the independent regulatory agencies issued 18 major rules in FY2013. Of those 18 rules, the agencies appear to have provided some information on either costs or benefits in 12 rules.[34]

Because most cost-benefit analysis requirements do not extend to the independent regulatory agencies, the bottom-up approach to estimating the costs and benefits of regulation does not include costs and benefits of regulations issued by those agencies. This includes, for example, many of the financial regulations issued pursuant to the Dodd-Frank Wall Street Reform and Consumer Protection Act of 2010, which are primarily issued by the financial regulators—most of which are excluded from the cost-benefit requirement of Executive Order 12866.[35] The exclusion of certain types of agencies from cost-benefit analysis requirements is a weakness in the annual OMB reports and presents a challenge to bottom-up approaches of estimating costs and benefits. The OMB reports generally identify the number of rules issued by independent regulatory agencies that provide some information on some costs and/or benefits, but they do not typically have information about the magnitude of those costs or benefits.

Costs and Benefit Estimates Only Required for Economically Significant Rules

Second, the agencies that are subject to cost-benefit analysis requirements are not required to conduct a cost-benefit analysis for every rule—only those rules that are deemed economically significant, as defined by Executive Order 12866. Specifically, the order defines economically significant rules as those that have an annual effect on the economy of at least $100 million. [36] Rules that are significant, but not economically significant, are subject to requirements for OIRA review and may have a less formal assessment of costs and benefits, but agencies are not generally required to conduct a complete cost-benefit assessment for those rules.[37] As such, the rules included in the OMB reports' total estimates of costs and benefits are only economically significant rules.[38]

Monetizing Costs Can Be Challenging

Third, quantifying and monetizing certain costs and benefits can be very difficult, and agencies do not often monetize all of the expected effects of their regulations. The bottom-up approach, however, is limited to totaling only those costs and benefits that are actually monetized. Under current rulemaking requirements, agencies are encouraged, but not necessarily required, to monetize costs and benefits.[39] For example, Executive Order 12866 states that agencies should provide a quantification of costs and benefits "to the extent feasible."[40]

Monetizing the effects of regulations involves converting expected effects, such as costs to consumers or changes to a population's health or behavior, into dollar terms. Monetizing the effects of regulations involves turning costs and benefits into a common unit—dollars—so that they can be compared against one another. This can allow for an evaluation of the cost-effectiveness of a rule, such as a calculation of the cost of each life expected to be saved by a rule, or the cost-benefit ratio of a rule.

Although some of the effects of a rule can be measured fairly easily in dollar terms, such as certain types of equipment or technologies for which a market value can be easily identified, other effects are more difficult to monetize. In cases in which dollar amounts are not readily available, agencies often rely on economic techniques that attempt to simulate market exchanges. One method agencies use to monetize certain concepts is based on a formula that includes monetized values known as "willingness-to-pay" or "willingness-to-accept" to measure the value that individuals place on the change resulting from a particular regulation.[41] This allows an agency to assign a dollar value to a regulatory outcome that may not otherwise have an easily identifiable value, and then the estimate can be compared against the costs of obtaining that benefit. For example, agencies sometimes use the "value of a statistical life" or "VSL" to assign a monetized amount to the benefits per life saved from certain types of regulations.[42] The agency can then compare this monetized estimate of benefits against the costs of the rule to see whether the rule's costs were justified by its benefits.

The executive orders and OMB guidance documents recognize that quantification and monetization can be difficult in some cases and allow agencies some flexibility in determining when effects can be quantified and monetized:

- Executive Order 12866 instructs agencies to provide information on the quantified costs of the anticipated costs and benefits of regulations "to the extent feasible."[43]
- OMB Circular A-4, which OMB issued in 2003 to provide guidance to agencies on how to conduct cost-benefit analysis, states that agencies "should develop quantitative estimates and convert them to dollar amounts if possible. In many cases, quantified estimates are readily convertible, with a little effort, into dollar equivalents."[44]
- Executive Order 13563, which President Obama issued in January 2011, stated that "Where appropriate and permitted by law, each agency may consider (and discuss qualitatively) values that are difficult or impossible to quantify, including equity, human dignity, fairness, and distributive impacts." [45]
- OMB's 2011 guidance document, "Regulatory Impact Analysis: A Primer," instructs agencies to quantify the costs and benefits in terms of units—for example, the number of premature deaths avoided each year or the number of prevented nonfatal illnesses—as well as monetizing the costs and benefits associated with each of these effects, to the extent possible.[46]

As OMB explained in its 2014 report,

> When agencies have not quantified or monetized the primary benefits or costs of regulations, it is generally because of conceptual and empirical challenges, including an absence of relevant information. Many rules have benefits or costs that cannot be quantified or monetized with existing information, and the aggregate estimates presented here do not capture those non-monetized benefits and costs. In some cases, quantification of various effects is highly speculative. For example, it may not be possible to quantify the benefits of certain disclosure requirements, even if those benefits are likely to be large, simply because the impact of some of these requirements cannot be specified in advance.[47]

Practitioners or observers of the rulemaking process do not necessarily agree on what effects are appropriate to monetize. For example, the Obama Administration has placed greater emphasis than earlier Administrations on the value of qualitative benefits such as equity and dignity.[48] Debates in the literature have raised questions over when it may be appropriate to quantify or monetize certain qualitative effects of rules. For example, questions have been raised as to whether dignity and other psychological effects of rules, such as fear and anxiety, should be monetized in regulatory impact analyses.[49]

In sum, to achieve an accurate assessment of the total costs and benefits of regulations in dollar terms using a bottom-up method, one would have to monetize all possible effects of regulation, and such an undertaking is not consistent with current rulemaking requirements or practice. OMB did state in its 2014 report, however, that OMB believes "the benefits and costs of major rules, which have the largest economic effects, account for the majority of the total benefits and costs of all rules subject to OMB review."[50]

Given that agencies do not estimate cost and benefits for every rule issued in every year, estimates that use the bottom-up approach are likely under-reporting costs and benefits. On the other hand, as discussed more below, some of the literature evaluating the quality and accuracy of cost-benefit analyses has suggested that costs and benefits for rules evaluated are overestimated by agencies.

Potential Uncertainties in Individual Cost-Benefit Analyses

Cost-benefit estimates are produced by agencies to assist with decisionmaking in individual rules, and the estimates often contain some uncertainty from not knowing precisely the potential effects of rules. For example, consider a rule in which an agency conducts a risk assessment, such as an airline safety rule intended to lower the risk of a terrorist attack on the United States. The estimate of costs and benefits for this rule would contain a great deal of underlying uncertainty, because precisely estimating the projected decrease in the risk of a terrorist attack and the precise cost of the rule is likely impossible. On the other hand, a rule that would result in changes that can be more easily predicted and measured, such as a rule requiring the purchase of new safety equipment for a vehicle fleet, is likely to contain less uncertainty.

To attempt to reduce uncertainty and produce high-quality, robust estimates, current requirements and guidance documents encourage agencies to base their estimates on the best reasonable obtainable scientific, technical, and economic information. With regard to uncertainties, agencies are instructed to analyze and present them as part of the overall regulatory analysis.[51] This generally results in the agencies producing a range of estimates of costs and benefits and using certain types of analytical techniques (e.g., sensitivity analysis) to identify how benefits and costs of a rule would change due to changes in key variables.

As stated in a 1996 article outlining the challenges of uncertainty in cost-benefit analysis (also referred to as benefit-cost analysis),

> Benefit-cost analysis can help decision-makers better understand the implications of decisions by identifying and, where appropriate, quantifying the favorable and unfavorable consequences of a proposed policy change, even when information on benefits and costs, is highly uncertain. In some cases, however, benefit-cost analysis cannot be used to conclude that the economic benefits of a decision will exceed or fall short of its costs, because there is simply too much uncertainty.[52]

In adding the results of all the individual studies together, however, the context and uncertainties of each individual study may be lost. As OMB stated in its first report on costs and benefits,

> Studies that have attempted to total up the total costs and benefits of Federal regulations have basically added together a diverse set of individual studies. Unfortunately, these individual studies vary in quality, methodology, and type of regulatory costs included. Thus we have an apples and oranges problem, or, more aptly, an apples, oranges, kiwis, grapefruit, etc., problem.[53]

Adding together existing estimates of costs and benefits treats the individual estimates as though they are precise estimates, but they may be imprecise estimates. "CBA can sometimes produce an illusion of certainty," as one former OIRA Administrator stated. This illusion of certainty can be misleading in individual cost and benefits estimates, and it becomes even more so when such estimates are aggregated. [54] In any individual estimate of costs and benefits, "numerous technical judgments must be made, and technical analysts might well disagree."[55] Aggregating all of the bottom-up estimates that agencies have produced can cause the context and any important caveats or reflections of uncertainty in each regulatory impact analysis to be lost.

Questions Over Accuracy of Individual Cost and Benefit Estimates

Uncertainty in how best to estimate costs and benefits leads to the question of whether the results are *accurate*—i.e., whether agencies overestimate or underestimate costs and benefits. Proponents of regulation tend to argue that agencies overestimate costs of regulation.[56] On the other hand, opponents of regulations tend to argue that agencies underestimate costs—agencies may have incentives to underestimate the costs of regulations and overestimate the benefits, which would help to make the case for promulgating a regulation because of its positive net benefits.[57] To address this important question, a number of studies have examined the accuracy of agency estimates of costs and benefits. One academic study published in 2000 compared *ex ante* studies to *ex post* studies and found that agencies frequently overestimated both costs and benefits of regulations.[58] In 2010, the same authors performed a similar *ex post* study of several cost-benefit estimates that had been produced by agencies subsequent to their 2000 study. Again, they concluded that regulatory agencies tended to overestimate the total costs of regulations, explaining that "a variety of factors contribute to initial government agency cost estimates that may differ from the realized results, although in some cases this is coincident with differences in benefits produced by regulations."[59]

In its 2005 report to Congress on the costs and benefits of regulations, OMB included a chapter on "validation" of cost estimates.[60] OMB examined a number of *ex ante* cost-benefit estimates and compared them with *ex post* estimates, when they were available.[61] OMB's conclusions were that the costs of regulations were more often overestimated by the agency, but that the benefits were sometimes overestimated as well.

A primary reason observers have given for the overestimation of costs is that agencies tend to underestimate industry's ability to innovate, and therefore compliance with regulations sometimes turns out to be less costly than expected. The ability to adapt to regulatory requirements and identify more cost-effective methods of meeting compliance targets can result in lower compliance costs than initially anticipated by the agency. For example, consider the Environmental Protection Agency's acid rain (sulfur dioxide) program in the 1990s. Mandated under the Clean Air Act Amendments of 1990, the EPA issued regulations aimed at reducing sulfur dioxide emissions. Studies suggest that the EPA's initial cost estimates for these regulations were too high due to EPA's underestimation of how industry would adapt and find less costly means of achieving the reduction targets. In sum, as stated in one retrospective study, "When forecasting the costs of new environmental regulations, economic analysts have routinely ignored a primary economic lesson: Markets will cut costs through innovation."[62]

A number of other reasons may contribute to inaccuracies in agency estimates of costs. For example, delays in implementation of regulations can help lower the compliance costs as it can allow industry more time to identify cost-effective solutions.[63] Over- or under-estimating certain effects of regulations can also result in inaccuracies, such as compliance rates among regulated entities. Finally, agencies first estimate costs and benefits while writing the proposed regulation, but the regulation may change in response to comments received during the public comment period.[64] As regulations are revised in response to comments, cost-benefit estimates are not always updated. Changes made in the rule after it has been proposed and before it is finalized could affect the likely costs and benefits of the rule—for example, if the final rule sets a standard that is less stringent as compared to the proposed rule, it will probably be less costly to comply.

In short, the accuracy of the bottom-up approach relies heavily on the precision of the individual cost and benefit estimates, but the accuracy of these estimates is likely to vary.

Measuring Costs over Time

Another issue in aggregating the costs and benefits of individual regulations is identification of the appropriate time period. In other words, how many years' worth of regulations should be included in the total? Regulations issued many years ago typically still have some compliance costs, although the cost of complying with regulations is generally thought to decrease over time. For example, if compliance with a new regulation requires industry to invest in new types of technology, once these investments have been made, the majority of the costs may already have been incurred, and the ongoing costs will be less. The time frame under which these compliance costs are distributed varies among rules. Similarly, the distribution of benefits can vary widely as well, and benefits of regulations often are not realized until the regulation has been in place for some time. For example, this is typically the case with regulations that have health benefits, such as environmental regulations that are intended to improve air quality.

Individual cost estimates of regulations are calculated by comparing the anticipated effects of a regulation against what would be expected to happen in a world without the regulation. These *ex ante* estimates that are conducted prior to the issuance of the regulation are usually the sole source of information on regulations' costs. Under current requirements and practice, an ongoing monitoring of the costs and benefits of rules is not required once a regulation has been issued.

The annual OMB reports have typically included 10 years' worth of cost and benefit estimates. According to the 2014 report, "OMB chose a ten-year period for aggregation because pre-regulation estimates prepared for rules adopted more than ten years ago are of questionable relevance today."[65] Similar reasons are cited in earlier versions of the OMB reports.

In its 2014 report, OMB acknowledges this weakness in its approach, stating that because the estimates do not include non-major rules or rules issued more than 10 years ago, the total costs and benefits currently in effect are like to be "significantly larger" than the totals in the report.[66] Over time, however, measuring the effects of those rules issued more than 10 years ago will become increasingly difficult. As stated in a 2006 study that discussed OMB's practice of including 10 years' worth of costs and benefits in its annual reports,

> If the regulation only requires small changes in behavior over a small time interval, then analysts feel confident of estimating the cost, hypothetical or not. But as the size or time interval increases, the shadow of the hypothetical looms ever larger. To take an extreme example, how would be begin to estimate the cost of federal child labor laws that were enacted during the 1930s?[67]

It is certainly the case that some rules that are more than 10 years old still impose a cost, and therefore this 10-year rule may result in a lower estimate of total costs over time because it excludes those rules. However, some cutoff probably should be made, as including estimates for costs of regulations made more than 10 years ago becomes less practicable.

These potential flaws have led some to attempt to use an entirely different approach to estimating the effects of regulations: the top-down method, which is discussed next.[68]

"Top-Down" Method: Estimating Costs Using Macroeconomic Modeling

Some scholars have adopted an approach to estimating the costs of rules that is referred to as a top-down approach. This section explains and analyzes the top-down approach, using a case study as an illustration for several of the concepts discussed.

What Is the Top-Down Approach?

The top-down approach uses macroeconomic variables and modeling techniques to measure the effect of regulation on the economy as a whole. Rather than aggregating existing cost estimates, the top-down method uses the results of an economic model that has been used to measure the relationship between the size of an economy, or economic growth, and some proxy of the level of regulation in a country, to measure the economic effects of regulation. This method typically compares the U.S. economy, as measured by some variable such as gross domestic product (GDP), to a hypothetical scenario in which the U.S. has less regulation. The approach takes the difference in the GDP under these two scenarios—the status quo and the scenario with less regulation—and calculates the change in GDP that might occur were the U.S. to reduce its overall amount of regulation. This potential change in GDP is considered to be the cost of regulation under the top-down approach and is explained in further detail below.

Why Use the Top-Down Approach?

The benefits of using a top-down approach, in many ways, are opposite from the bottom-up approach described above. Because the top-down approach uses measurements of various economic factors, it incorporates broader, more indirect effects that are not included in the bottom-up approach. This could include indirect economic effects, as well as direct effects that are not monetized.

Case Study: Crain and Crain Report

A commonly cited study using the top-down approach to totaling the cost of regulation is entitled "The Cost of Federal Regulation to the U.S. Economy, Manufacturing and Small Business," by W. Mark Crain and Nicole V. Crain, and it was most recently released in September 2014.[69]

The Crain and Crain report estimates the total cost of regulation and also explores the distribution of those regulatory costs among regulated entities. The component of the report that is most discussed in the debate over regulatory reform is the estimate of the total cost of regulation.[70] Hence, this CRS report focuses primarily on the components of the studies that describe the total cost of regulation, and not on the portion of the report exploring the distribution of costs among different types of firms.[71]

The Crain and Crain estimate of the total cost of regulation is not a purely top-down measure of the cost of regulations. It combines a top-down estimate—their estimate of the cost of economic regulation—with a bottom-up estimate of environmental, tax compliance, occupational safety, and homeland security regulation. However, the estimate of the cost of economic regulation resulting from their top-down methodology is almost 75% of the total estimate, totaling $1.439 trillion out of $2.028 trillion in the 2014 study. This report only discusses that portion of their estimate, as it is the most widely cited top-down study in the regulatory reform debate, and therefore serves as a useful example for discussion.

Background on the Crain and Crain Report

The 2014 Crain and Crain report can be traced back to a report originally published in 1995 by Thomas D. Hopkins for the Small Business Administration's (SBA's) Office of Advocacy entitled "Profiles of Regulatory Costs."[72] Each of the studies from 1995 through 2010 was prepared for the Office of Advocacy.

In the 1995 study, Hopkins estimated annual federal regulatory costs to be in the range of $416 billion to $668 billion in 1995. Six years later, in 2001, W. Mark Crain and Hopkins issued a follow-up to the 1995 Hopkins study, estimating the total annual cost of regulations to be $843 billion in 2000.[73] In 2005, Crain estimated annual regulatory costs to be about $1.1 trillion in 2004.[74] In 2010, Nicole V. Crain and W. Mark Crain issued another version of the study, which estimated the total cost of regulation to be $1.75 trillion in 2008. They explained the increase from $1.1 trillion in the 2005 report to $1.75 trillion as being, in part, the result of "new methodological techniques," meaning that "direct comparisons to the results in their prior studies should be made with caution."[75]

A number of concerns were raised about the methodology used in the 2010 report—and primarily the methods used to arrive at the $1.75 trillion of the total cost of regulation. Some of the entities raising concerns included the Office of Advocacy itself, the entity that had granted the contract under which the study was conducted. For example, the Office of Advocacy posted a number of caveats on its website where the report was linked, stating that "the findings of the study have been taken out of context and certain theoretical estimates of costs have been presented publicly as verifiable facts."[76] A 2011 CRS report called into question the methods used in the report to arrive at the total estimate of the cost of federal regulation.[77] A 2014 Government Accountability Office (GAO) report also raised issues with the study related to federal data quality standards, asserting that the Office of Advocacy failed to uphold those standards.[78]

Summary of the 2014 Crain and Crain Report

The 2014 Crain and Crain study estimated the total cost of federal regulation to be $2.028 trillion in 2012 (in 2014 dollars), an amount equal to 12% of U.S. GDP. This section summarizes the methodology used to arrive at this estimate, so that the estimate may be used as an illustration throughout the rest of the discussion of the top-down methodology.[79]

As mentioned above, economic regulation is the majority of the total cost of the Crain and Crain estimate: $1.448 trillion.[80] According to Crain and Crain, economic regulations are those that

> "govern decision-making in market transactions. These include markets for final goods and services; markets for physical and human resources; credit markets; and markets for the transport and delivery of products and factors of production."[81]

To arrive at this estimate of the total cost of economic regulation, Crain and Crain conducted a cross-country comparison of 34 Organization for Economic Cooperation and Development (OECD) countries, including the United States. Specifically, they looked at the relationship between each country's economy and a proxy measure of the amount of regulation in each country over eight years. The data Crain and Crain used for this proxy measure were derived from the World Economic Forum's Global Competitiveness Report.[82]

Crain and Crain used three components of the Global Competitiveness Index, a component of the Global Competitiveness Report that measures various aspects of the institutions, policies, and factors that determine a country's level of productivity. These types of measures are sometimes referred to as governance indicators. The report uses an "Executive Opinion Survey," which captures the opinions of business leaders around the world to construct a number of its indicators. Crain and Crain selected three indicators, each of which was constructed using the survey, to represent the amount of economic regulation in each country. The three indicators were

- burden of government regulation;
- efficiency of legal framework in challenging regulation; and
- regulation of securities exchanges.[83]

The survey respondents provided a value for each of these indicators ranging from one to seven. As Crain and Crain explained in their report, "higher values correspond to improvements in regulatory quality—that is, reductions in the regulatory burden on product, factor and credit markets."[84] To construct their measure for each country and each year, Crain and Crain used the mean value of these three factors. The regulation index that Crain and Crain used combined these three factors into a single measure for each of the countries in each of the years for which the data were available—2006 to 2013.

Using the mean value for the 34 countries over their eight-year period, Crain and Crain estimated a regression model in which they measured the effect of a number of variables—with their primary variable of interest being the measure of regulatory quality—on GDP per capita. The other variables, or "control" variables, were foreign trade as a share of GDP, population over 65 relative to population aged 19 to 65 (the "dependency ratio"), new capital investment as a share of GDP, size of the labor force, and tax revenues as a share of GDP.[85]

Based on the results of the regression model, Crain and Crain concluded that the effect of their purported proxy of economic regulation on GDP per capita was statistically significant. Further, they used the results of the regression model to estimate the total cost of the index on the GDP per capita in the United States. To do so, they compared the U.S. score on the regulation index with the average score of the five top performing (i.e., highest ranked) countries on the scale, which they referred to as the "benchmark countries." They used this "benchmark" measure as a hypothetical measurement of what a lower level of regulation in the United States could be. The difference between the U.S. score and the benchmark countries' average score was 26%.

Crain and Crain concluded that this 26% difference in the regulation index in the United States "implies an impact on GDP equal to $1.439 trillion. In other words, if the burden of economic regulation in the United States matched the benchmark countries, U.S. GDP would be $1.439 trillion higher than it was in 2012."[86] To the $1.439 trillion estimate, Crain and Crain added another $8.3 billion, which was the estimated cost of import restrictions from the U.S. International Trade Commission.[87] The total estimate of the cost of economic regulation they arrived at using this methodology was $1.448 trillion.

Analysis of Top-Down Approach to Estimating Costs and Benefits

A number of issues have been raised with the top-down approach, some of which are explained below using the Crain and Crain study as an illustration.

Importance of Accurate Measures of Regulation in Top-Down Approach

One challenge for the top-down approach to estimating the cost of regulation is that the accuracy of the findings is dependent on the validity of the proxy measure of regulation. The proxy is used to model the relationship between the size of the economy and amount of regulation, and then the parameter estimates resulting from the model are used to calculate the total cost of economic regulation.

Identifying an accurate measure of regulation, however, is a challenge. As explained in a report by the Council on Foreign Relations (CFR) on federal rulemaking policy in the United States and other countries, as well as in previous CRS reports, quantifying the total amount of regulation is an inherently difficult task.[88] As stated in the CFR report,

> Economists have not settled on a good way to measure overall regulatory burden ... Because of these data limitations, the best empirical studies take on a specific regulation rather than the full stock of regulations. Largely unknown is how the average business is affected by the cumulative set of regulations, or whether certain regulations harm or help different kinds of business activity, such as innovation or entrepreneurship.[89]

Obtaining an accurate proxy measure of regulation is key in any economic model that uses regulation as an explanatory variable, because an inaccurate measure can introduce serious uncertainty into the model's results. The term economists use to refer to whether a measure of a construct correctly represents what it purports to represent is "content validity." To illustrate the importance of content validity in the top-down approach of measuring the cost of regulation, this section will more closely examine the measure of "regulatory quality" used by Crain and Crain.

Crain and Crain referred to their measure of regulatory quality as the "Economic Regulation Index." They created the index from data from the World Economic Forum's (WEF's) annual Global Competitiveness Report—specifically, the report's Executive Opinion Survey.[90] In that survey, the WEF captured the opinions of over 13,000 business leaders in 148 different economies during a five-month period. Most of the survey questions, including the three used in the Crain and Crain study to measure regulation, involved rating on a scale of one to seven a particular aspect of the operating environment in the respondent's country. The questions covered such topics as innovation and technology infrastructure, education and human capital, and tourism. To create a measure of regulation from this survey, Crain and Crain selected three questions, each of which included an explicit reference to regulation (which appears to be how they selected them): (1) burden of government regulation, (2) efficiency of legal framework in challenging regulation, and (3) regulation of securities exchanges.

Are these three questions from the Executive Opinion Survey measuring this type of specific regulation—in other words, can the responses to these three questions be considered a useful proxy of the burden of economic regulation? This may be difficult to answer, but it is crucial to the validity of the study's conclusions. Crain and Crain state that "the reach of economic regulations is vast. This means that an encompassing methodology is required to derive an estimate of these costs."[91] While their statement about the vastness of economic regulation is certainly true, whether their measurement and methodology measures it accurately is difficult to validate.[92]

Proxy measures of governance indicators are inherently imprecise, and they cannot be reliably used to estimate macroeconomic outcomes. A recent article examining a similar cross-country set of indicators illustrates the difficulty in identifying an accurate measure for certain inherently abstract concepts related to governance, such as the "rule of law," or, in this case, regulation.[93] The article specifically focused on the World Bank's "Worldwide Governance Indicators" (WGI), though it argued that "the concerns raised here about the WGI apply equally to other current governance indicators."[94] The article stated that "both researchers and policymakers should require evidence that governance indicators are valid before employing them. In the absence of such evidence, research results obtained using such indicators are uninterpretable and should not survive peer review. For policymakers, reliance on such indicators would be arbitrary."[95] It could be argued that the use of such indicators in the top-down model of total cost of regulation may suffer from this problem of questionable measurement.

Specific concerns over this issue as it relates to top-down studies involving regulation were raised in 2010 over the Crain and Crain report and arguably still apply to the 2014 report as well, due to the similarities of their measures. For example, economist Art Kraay, one of the creators of the World

Bank's Regulatory Quality Index, the measure of regulation that Crain and Crain used in their 2010 study, commented in response to their study that the measure of regulatory quality they created measured the perceptions of various regulatory environments, rather than the stringency of those environments.[96] The index used in the 2014 study uses a different proxy, although its construction was similar—it measures business leaders' *perceptions* of the regulatory environment in various countries.[97] Some research suggests that there may be key differences between perceptions of something and actual levels of it, however:

> There is a substantial difference between measuring a thing and measuring perceptions of it. In the context of governance, for example, perceptions of crime risk have been shown to be quite different than actual crime levels (see, for example, Forgas, 1980; Pfeiffer, 2005); perceptions of corruption have been shown to differ from actual corruption levels (see, for example, Olken, 2006; Seligson, 2006); and trust in government has been shown to differ from administrative performance (Van de Walle and Bouckaert, 2007).[98]

In sum, this question of whether a measurement based on survey responses of business leaders or other individuals, such as the Executive Opinion Survey, is measuring what it purports to measure, is an important one. With any top-down model of the economic effects of regulation, the validity of a proxy for regulation is essential—and measuring an inherently abstract concept like the stringency of regulation in a country is difficult. Without a valid proxy, which is difficult to identify for the reasons discussed above (and possibly others), the findings of any top-down study could be brought into question.

Questions About Proper Model Specification

Setting aside the question of how to undertake the difficult task of measuring regulation, and assuming that the measure of regulation is a valid measurement, another crucial question remains for the top-down approach to measuring the cost of regulation: how should one select the right model?

In a regression model, such as the one used by Crain and Crain, a researcher is attempting to explain a relationship between variables by analyzing the extent to which the dependent variable can be explained by changes in the independent variables. Proper selection of all variables in the model is important, as discussed below.

Selecting Independent Variables

Selecting and including the proper independent and control variables in an econometric analysis is crucial to the validity of the model's results. For example, a researcher must include all variables that are thought to be theoretically relevant and take care not to omit variables that may help explain the outcome.[99] Explaining and theoretically justifying the components of economic models, including all independent variables, is important: "It is critical that researchers explain and justify the assumptions that underlie their model, which are presumed to be informed by theory."[100]

Failure to include all relevant variables in an economic model can result in omitted variable bias. Omitted variable bias can occur when one of the explanatory variables—those variables in the model that are helping to explain changes in the dependent variable—has its effects overstated because a variable that is related to that variable has been left out of the model. In other words, the omitted variable's explanatory power will be attributed to the variable that is included in the model, as long as the two variables are correlated. As explained in one study,

> Because top-down methods [of estimating the cost of regulation] associate indicators of regulatory activity with changes in macroeconomic variables, they risk attributing to regulation the effects of other variables that are not considered in the analysis but that may be correlated with regulatory activity. There is a strong chance of omitted variable bias, in other words.[101]

In sum, were a top-down model of regulation to leave out some relevant variables, the effect of regulation could be overstated.

Selecting a Dependent Variable

Furthermore, identifying a theoretically sound dependent variable is crucial to the validity of a model's results. Crain and Crain used GDP per capita as their dependent variable, rather than GDP growth rate. Measuring GDP per capita does provide an indication of the size of a country's economy. However, it can potentially be problematic because it ignores the historical circumstances that have led each country's economy to its current size, and therefore it presumes to explain the current size of each economy only based upon the factors in the model. Using the rate of GDP growth instead of GDP per capita would presume that the *changes* in the size of each country's economy are explained by the independent variables, not the actual size of the economy itself—which could be considered more likely.

Selecting the Correct Form

Another important issue related to model specification is whether the nature of the relationship between the dependent variable and the independent variables is properly specified: in other words, is the relationship linear or nonlinear? A linear relationship in expressed on a graph with a straight line and assumes that the *rate* of change in the dependent variable does not vary—hence the straight line on a graph. A non-linear relationship can also be expressed on a graph but does not have a straight line, and it assumes that the rate of change in the dependent variable *can* change. These concepts are discussed more below in the context of the top-down approach. Notably, however, identifying the form of the relationship between dependent and independent variables is important—"the consequences of an incorrect functional form for interpretation and forecasting can be severe."[102]

Crain and Crain ran a linear regression, which is based upon the assumption that the relationship is of direct proportionality and is expressed on a graph with a straight line.[103] Whether this is the type of relationship between regulation and size of a country's economy, or its economic growth generally, is an important question. Crain and Crain did not appear to provide a theoretical basis for assuming the relationship is linear, and some scholars have suggested that the relationship between regulation and economic growth is nonlinear. A 2012 working paper from the George Washington University Regulatory Studies Center suggested that "perhaps... up to a point, increasing the size of government may tend to increase GDP, but that the relationship reverses after a certain threshold."[104] That paper examined whether a measure of the on-budget costs of federal regulation in the United States had an effect on GDP growth, which is a different objective than a top-down model of the cost of regulation, but it illustrates the important point that some effects on GDP can be nonlinear. If such model misspecification did occur in the Crain and Crain model, the results of their model could be held in question.

In sum, these three issues related to model specification—selection of independent variables, selection of dependent variables, and selection of the correct functional form for the model—are highly important to the reliability and validity of conclusions made based upon a top-down estimate of the cost of regulation.

Other Potential Methodological Issues

There are several additional methodological issues that may be of concern in the top-down approach, including unclear directions of causality and insufficient sample size in the model.

Questions of Causality

The first issue, which is linked to the question of identification of a dependent variable, relates to questions of causality in a top-down approach that uses a measure of regulation to explain the health of a country's economy: does the amount of regulation affect the economy, or could the economy also have an effect on the amount of regulation? This uncertainty about the direction of the causality between different components of a model is referred to by economists as "endogeneity." The presence of endogeneity can cause bias in the parameter estimates resulting from the model. As mentioned earlier in this report, it is crucial that researchers using a top-down approach explain the theory behind all of the components of their models. Having a solid theoretical foundation related to the causality question can reduce or eliminate the likelihood that a model will suffer from endogeneity.

In the case of top-down studies of regulation like Crain and Crain, the parameter estimates are used to calculate the potential difference in GDP, which is the estimate that Crain and Crain provide for the cost of economic regulation. As explained in the section above summarizing their methodology, Crain and Crain assert that the GDP per capita is a direction function of the amount of regulation in a country. They do not explore the possibility that the causality could also go in the other direction. The presence of such endogeneity can cause the results of the model to be incorrect.

The issue of correctly identifying the causal relationship is a challenge for scholars examining the relationship between regulation and other macroeconomic factors. For example, a recent study of the "regulatory volume" in states across the United States "looked at the relationship between regulatory output and a series of indicators described above meant to represent the economic health of the state." The study concluded that "citizens in more prosperous states may very well demand more regulation than citizens in less prosperous states."[105] A similar concern could potentially be raised about the direction of causality between the volume of regulation and the economy.

Sample Size

The second is an issue of sample size, particularly for a top-down study that uses a cross-country comparison of industrialized economies. A small sample size can have detrimental effects on the precision of the model's results: a smaller sample size makes the estimate less precise and therefore less reliable. Researchers who examine cross-country comparisons of regulation face some potential problems, including the small number of fully industrialized countries and the fairly short length of time over which regulatory measures have been constructed.

The Crain and Crain study uses 34 countries and a time period of eight years: 2006 to 2013. This is a relatively small sample size, especially given that the measures of regulation and other variables in the model are unlikely to change very much from one year to the next in just an eight-year period.[106] In addition, this specific eight-year period is not necessarily a typical one, as it is the period leading up to and immediately following the Great Recession.[107] Therefore, conclusions made based upon this narrow time period may not be generalizable to other years or other periods.[108]

Potential for Double-Counting Costs

In the top-down approach, another potential problem is whether costs may be double-counted. Crain and Crain separate their total estimate of the cost of regulations into four categories, as described above, although it appears that this approach may be double-counting the cost of some regulations for at least two reasons.

The first reason is an econometric one: as mentioned above, the potential for omitted variable bias exists in any econometric model. If Crain and Crain omitted a variable that is highly correlated with their measure of "economic" regulations—such as a measure of environmental or other types of regulations, which are almost undoubtedly correlated with their measure of economic regulation—then the explanatory power of the omitted variable becomes attributed to the coefficient on the economic regulation measure. In other words, the explanatory strength of that measure is inflated by the omission of other variables that are not included. By adding other measures of regulation, including environmental regulations, to the total cost they estimate for economic regulation, Crain and Crain may therefore be double-counting the effects of these other types of regulations.

Second, the potential for double-counting exists because of the nature of the questions asked to business leaders that comprise the regulatory quality measure. The questions themselves do not necessarily measure *only* economic regulation, although Crain and Crain imply that to be the case. Rather, as discussed above, they measure potentially very broad effects of all types of regulation by measuring the overall regulatory environment. Because Crain and Crain is a hybrid study that also employs a bottom-up methodology to measure certain types of regulation, they add an estimate of the cost of other types of regulation to their estimate of the cost of economic regulation. As a result, their overall number of roughly $2 trillion could include some double counting.[109]

No Discussion of Benefits of Regulations

To date, it appears that the top-down approach has not been used to estimate benefits of regulation—only costs. It is not clear whether the method *could* be used to measure benefits, because the approach measures cost in terms of potential economic growth that has not occurred due to the amount of regulation. A parallel approach does not seem to be applicable to benefits, which, as discussed above, are often not easily measured in dollar amounts or economic effects, and therefore may not be able to be estimated in this same way.

Although the top-down method does not appear to be intended to measure costs *and* benefits, having an estimate of costs without an estimate of benefits does not provide the complete context for evaluating whether a country's amount of regulation is appropriate. Such a comparison of costs against benefits has been institutionalized in the regulatory process in the United States since the early 1980s. Specifically, one of the underlying components of the current regulatory system, which was formally put into place by President Ronald Reagan in 1981 when he issued Executive Order 12291, is that agencies should consider the costs of individual regulations and compare them against the benefits, and that "regulatory action shall not be undertaken unless the potential benefits to society for the regulation outweigh the potential costs to society."[110] This general approach of comparing costs against benefits has been upheld since the Reagan Administration formalized it in 1981, and the shift to become more reliant on estimates of costs and benefits in informing regulatory decisions over the past several decades has been well documented.[111]

In sum, the notion that costs and benefits must be compared to one another has remained a crucial component of the regulatory process in the United States over the past several decades. Under current rulemaking requirements, agencies are responsible for measuring costs against benefits in individual regulations, and because of the nature of the bottom-up method and its reliance on those estimates, it can be used to make overall comparisons between total costs and benefits. Such a comparison does not seem possible, however, at the macroeconomic level.

SUMMARY: ADVANTAGES AND DISADVANTAGES OF TWO APPROACHES

Each of the two main approaches taken to estimate the total costs and benefits of regulations have pros and cons, which tend to mirror one another. This final section briefly compares the two approaches and provides some perspective on why this issue is of potential interest to Congress.

The bottom-up approach to estimating the total costs and benefits of regulations, such as the approach taken by OMB in its annual report to Congress, has several advantages. The bottom-up approach involves adding up actual cost estimates calculated by agencies pursuant to rulemaking requirements. These estimates are conducted on an individual basis for certain regulations, and, although they often contain some uncertainty, are based upon specialized information the agency has regarding expected costs and benefits.

Notably, current requirements for agencies to estimate costs and benefits of their rules are intended to assist with agency decisionmaking in *individual* regulations by more fully informing decisionmakers of the likely outcomes and providing a means of evaluating and comparing regulatory alternatives. The potential utility of that information when taken out of the context of individual rules and aggregated, however, is greatly reduced.

An individual cost-benefit analysis conducted by an agency and included in the bottom-up aggregated estimate could also suffer from econometric problems similar to those described above in the context of the top-down approach. However, the individual estimates used in the bottom-up approach can be validated by comparing the *ex ante* estimates of costs and benefits to *ex post* estimates. Some such studies exist and are discussed above. In addition, agencies may— though they are not explicitly required to—revisit the original cost-benefit estimate when conducting a retrospective review of their regulations.[112] This provides a potential means of validating the results of the bottom-up method, whereas the top-down method does not have a similar opportunity for *ex post* validation.

The biggest potential problem with the bottom-up approach, however, is that the aggregated estimate is unlikely to represent the costs and benefits of all rules. Not all rules are included in the aggregate, because cost-benefit estimates are not currently conducted or required for all regulations. Furthermore, even for rules in which a cost-benefit analysis is required, monetizing certain types of costs and benefits can be challenging, and any effects of regulations that are not monetized are not able to be included in a bottom-up aggregate.

Because of these limitations about what may be missing from the bottom-up estimate, a top-down approach may be more likely to capture fully the overall cost of regulations, as the top-down approach could conceivably provide a way to include in its estimate of indirect costs and effects of regulations that are not included in the bottom-up approach. However, the top-down approach has several potential problems when it comes to implementation, most of which are conceptual and methodological. Any estimates of the cost of regulation resulting from a top-down approach are entirely reliant on the validity of the model, identification of its components and structure, and the theory behind it. The validity of an estimate is especially reliant upon the validity of the proxy measure of regulation. In practice, overcoming these conceptual and methodological hurdles is difficult, if not impossible, meaning that the results of a top-down approach should be treated with a great deal of caution.

Finally, the top-down approach does not make a comparison of costs to benefits. Such a comparison appears to be outside the purpose of the top-down approach, but having both estimates of costs and benefits can provide a more complete representation of the cost-effectiveness of a country's regulation.

Issues for Congress

Because of the role Congress plays in delegating legislative authority to federal agencies to issue regulations, Congress has shown an interest in conducting oversight of those regulations, both for individual regulations and the regulatory system generally. One way for Congress to conduct oversight of the regulatory system as a whole is to monitor the total cost and benefits of federal regulation.

Inaccuracies in cost-benefit estimates conducted by agencies could have the effect of undermining public confidence in the regulatory process.[113] So, too, could a misunderstanding or over-reliance on estimates of the total cost of regulation that are not intended to be considered precise findings. For the reasons discussed throughout this report, both approaches to estimating the total cost of regulation have inherent—and potentially insurmountable—flaws. The true cost of regulation is incredibly difficult to estimate for the many reasons discussed in this report, and perhaps others as well. The discrepancy between the two approaches and their associated estimates raises the question of the utility of using such figures in the regulatory reform debate.

End Notes

[1] See CRS Report R43056, Counting Regulations: An Overview of Rulemaking, Types of Federal Regulations, and Pages in the Federal Register, by Maeve P. Carey for a more detailed discussion of the nature and quantity of regulations issued each year.

[2] For an overview of the federal rulemaking process, see CRS Report RL32240, The Federal Rulemaking Process: An Overview, coordinated by Maeve P. Carey.

[3] For example, in January 2015, the House of Representatives passed H.R. 185, the Regulatory Accountability Act of 2015, which would make several changes to the current rulemaking process, including instituting more extensive cost-benefit analysis requirements.

[4] For example, see U.S. Congress, House Committee on the Judiciary, Subcommittee on Courts, Commercial and Administrative Law, APA at 65: Is Reform Needed to Create Jobs, Promote Economic Growth, and Reduce Costs?, 112th Cong., 1st sess., February 28, 2011, 112-17 (Washington: GPO, 2011); and Business Roundtable, Using Cost-Benefit Analysis To Create Smart Regulation: A Primer and Key Considerations for Congress and Federal Agencies, December 2014, http://businessroundtable.org/sites/default/files/reports/BRT%20Cost-Benefit%20Analysis.pdf.

[5] See, for example, the debate over rulemaking "ossification," which suggests that the addition of analytical requirements—along with other procedural requirements—has slowed the rulemaking process. See Thomas O. McGarity, "Some Thoughts on 'Deossifying' the Rulemaking Process," Duke Law Journal, vol. 41, no. 6 (June 1992), pp. 1385-1462; Jason Webb Yackee and Susan Webb Yackee, "Administrative Procedures and Bureaucratic Performance: Is Federal Rule-making 'Ossified'?" Journal of Public Administration Research and Theory, vol. 20 (2010), pp. 261-282; and Richard J. Pierce, Jr., "Rulemaking Ossification Is Real: A Response to Testing the Ossification Thesis," George Washington Law Review, vol. 80, no. 5 (July 2012), pp. 1493-1503.

[6] A proxy measure is a figure that is used to represent the value of something in a calculation or a model.

[7] To compare these figures, CRS adjusted the bottom-up numbers to be in 2014 dollars.

[8] For a detailed explanation of these requirements, see CRS Report R41974, Cost-Benefit and Other Analysis Requirements in the Rulemaking Process, coordinated by Maeve P. Carey.

[9] Executive Order 12866, "Regulatory Planning and Review," 58 Federal Register 51735, October 4, 1993. For more detailed information about this and other cost-benefit analysis requirements in the rulemaking process, see CRS Report R41974, Cost-Benefit and Other Analysis Requirements in the Rulemaking Process, coordinated by Maeve P. Carey.

[10] This requirement for cost-benefit analysis in Executive Order 12866 does not extend to the independent regulatory agencies listed at 44 U.S.C. § 3502(5), which includes, for example, the Federal Reserve and the Securities and Exchange Commission. For more information about the exclusion of the independent regulatory agencies from this cost-benefit analysis

requirement, see CRS Report R42821, Independent Regulatory Agencies, Cost-Benefit Analysis, and Presidential Review of Regulations, by Maeve P. Carey and Michelle D. Christensen.

[11] Executive Order 12866 § 3(f)(1).

[12] This phrase also includes transfer rules that transfer sums of over $100 million. For a more detailed analysis of the definition of "major" rules, see CRS Report R41651, REINS Act: Number and Types of "Major Rules" in Recent Years, by Maeve P. Carey and Curtis W. Copeland.

[13] For example, Section 1(b)(6) requires agencies to "assess both the costs and the benefits of the intended regulation and, recognizing that some costs and benefits are difficult to quantify, propose or adopt a regulation only upon a reasoned determination that the benefits of the intended regulation justify its costs." Section 1(b)(11) requires agencies to "tailor [their] regulations to impose the least burden on society," while "obtaining the regulatory objectives, taking into account, among other things, and to the extent practicable, the costs of cumulative regulations." These provisions are considered to be more like guiding principles, however, rather than specific requirements for cost-benefit analysis.

[14] Executive Order 13563, "Improving Regulations and Regulatory Review," 76 Federal Register 3821, January 21, 2011.

[15] For example, in 2003, OMB issued Circular A-4 to provide guidance to agencies on how to conduct cost-benefit analysis. See Office of Management and Budget, Circular A-4, "Regulatory Analysis," September 17, 2003, at http://www.whitehouse.gov/omb/assets/regulatory_matters_pdf/a-4.pdf. This guidance provides information such as what discount rates agencies should use, how to choose a time period for estimating future costs and benefits, etc. Since 2003, OMB has issued several additional guidance documents to provide instruction to agencies on complying with regulatory analysis requirements.

[16] The phrase "small entities" is considered in the RFA to include small businesses, local governments, and not-forprofit organizations. 5 U.S.C. §§601-612. For more information about requirements of the Regulatory Flexibility Act, see CRS Report RL34355, The Regulatory Flexibility Act: Implementation Issues and Proposed Reforms, coordinated by Maeve P. Carey.

[17] 2 U.S.C. §§1532-1538. For more information about UMRA, see CRS Report R40957, Unfunded Mandates Reform Act: History, Impact, and Issues, by Robert Jay Dilger and Richard S. Beth.

[18] Ex ante estimates are those conducted by agencies prior to a regulation being issued or taking effect, and they reflect the agency's prediction of what the effects of the regulation will be. Ex post estimates are done retrospectively—that is, after the regulation has been issued and taken effect—and they are used to evaluate the accuracy of the initial estimate and/or the effectiveness of the regulation.

[19] Government-wide retrospective reviews have been required since the Carter Administration, and most recently have been required by the Obama Administration in Executive Order 13563.

[20] See the section below entitled "Questions Over Accuracy of Individual Cost and Benefit Estimates" for an overview of this literature.

[21] These reports are available on OMB's website. See http://www.whitehouse.gov/omb/inforeg_regpol_reports_congress/.

[22] P.L. 104-208.

[23] P.L. 106-554, §1(a)(3) [title VI, §624], 114 Stat. 2763.

[24] The Draft 2015 report was released in October 2015, but had not yet been finalized as of the time of writing of this report.

[25] Office of Management and Budget, 2014 Report to Congress on the Benefits and Costs of Federal Regulations and Unfunded Mandates on State, Local, and Tribal Entities, available at https://www.whitehouse.gov/sites/default/files/omb/inforeg/2014_cb/2014-cost-benefit-report.pdf.

[26] The numbers cited here in this CRS report are inflation-adjusted to 2014 dollars. OMB reported the totals in both 2001 and 2010 dollars.

[27] As explained by OMB in the report, "budgetary transfer rules are rules that primarily cause income transfers usually from taxpayers to program beneficiaries" (p.8). Examples listed in the 2014 report included various education loan programs administered by the Department of Education, major capital investment projects administered by the Department of Transportation, and rules implementing the Supplemental Nutritional Assistance Program administered by the Department of Agriculture (see pp. 29-31 for a complete list of the major transfer rules).

[28] 2014 OMB Report, p. 8.

[29] The numbers cited here were inflation-adjusted by CRS to 2014 dollars. OMB reported the numbers in 2001 and 2010 dollars (see p. 24).

[30] It appears, though it is not entirely clear, that these numbers are reported in 2001 dollars (see p. 2). Adjusted for inflation to 2014 dollars, the estimated range of benefits for these two rules would be $648.8 million to $850.0 million.

[31] It appears, though it is not entirely clear, that these numbers are reported in 2001 dollars (see p. 2). Adjusted for inflation to 2014 dollars, the estimated range of costs for these 11 rules would be $2.1 billion to $3.1 billion.

[32] These agencies are listed at 44 U.S.C. 3502(5). When he issued Executive Order 12866, President Clinton chose not to include those agencies in the order's requirements for OMB review and cost-benefit analysis. President Reagan had made the same decision—to exclude the independent regulatory agencies—when he issued the predecessor order in 1981. See Executive Order 12291, "Federal Regulation," 46 Federal Register 13193, February 19, 1981. For more discussion of this decision, see CRS Report R42821, Independent Regulatory Agencies, Cost-Benefit Analysis, and Presidential Review of Regulations, by Maeve P. Carey and Michelle D. Christensen. For a discussion of characteristics of agency independence more generally, see CRS Report R43391, Independence of Federal Financial Regulators, by Henry B. Hogue, Marc Labonte, and Baird Webel, and CRS Report R43562, Administrative Law Primer: Statutory Definitions of "Agency" and Characteristics of Agency Independence, by Jared P. Cole and Daniel T. Shedd.

[33] For a more detailed discussion about what agency-specific requirements may apply to these agencies, see CRS Report R42821, Independent Regulatory Agencies, Cost-Benefit Analysis, and Presidential Review of Regulations, by Maeve P. Carey and Michelle D. Christensen, and Curtis W. Copeland, Economic Analysis and Independent Regulatory Agencies, report prepared for the consideration of the Administrative Conference of the United States, April 30, 2013, https://www.acus.gov/sites/default/files/documents/Copeland%20Final%20BCA%20Report%204-30-13.pdf.

[34] Office of Management and Budget, 2014 Report to Congress on the Benefits and Costs of Federal Regulations and Unfunded Mandates on State, Local, and Tribal Entities, available at https://www.whitehouse.gov/sites/default/files/omb/inforeg/2014_cb/2014-cost-benefit-report.pdf. In the table, the report indicates that seven rules have monetized costs and benefits, but it appears that the table may have added the numbers incorrectly.

[35] P.L. 111-203.

[36] Economically significant rules are those that may "have an annual effect on the economy of $100 million or more or adversely affect in a material way the economy, a sector of the economy, productivity, competition, jobs, the environment, public health or safety, or State, local, or tribal governments or communities" (Executive Order 12866 §3(f)(1)).

[37] Rules that are "significant" but not "economically significant" are required to undergo OMB review under Executive Order 12866. OMB's website, www.Reginfo.gov, provides data on the number of "significant" rules that OMB reviews each year (but not on the number of those rules that agencies issue each year). The data on OMB reviews show that the number of such rules reviewed each year is approximately in the range of 100-250; this is likely very similar to the number of such final rules issued each year.

[38] These rules are referred to in the OMB reports as "major" rules. Although the definitions of "major" rules and "economically significant" rules contain slight differences, the two terms are often used interchangeably.

[39] Under Executive Order 12866, the term "significant" rule encompasses a much broader number of rules than those considered "economically significant." For "significant" rules, agencies are asked to conduct an initial assessment of costs and benefits, but not a complete cost-benefit analysis.

[40] Executive Order 12866 §6(a)(3)(C)).

[41] In recent decades, as the use of cost-benefit analysis has increased, a debate has emerged about the appropriateness of monetizing certain costs and benefits in regulation. While economists generally favor the notion of assigning a monetized value to certain things like risks to life and health, others have opposed the monetization of certain effects of regulation. See, for example, W. Kip Viscusi, "Monetizing the Benefits of Risk and Environmental Regulation," Fordham Urban Law Journal, vol. 33, no. 4 (2005); W. Kip Viscusi, "What's to Know? Puzzles in the Literature on the Value of a Statistical Life," Journal of Economic Surveys, vol. 26, no. 5 (2011); and Robert W. Hahn, In Defense of the Economic Analysis of Regulation, (AEI Press, 2005). Others argue against this type of valuation; see Frank Ackerman and Lisa Heinzerling, Priceless: On Knowing the Price of Everything and the Value of Nothing (New York: The New Press, 2004).

[42] The VSL is calculated based upon a willingness-to-pay model. For example, if 100,000 people are willing to pay $60 to eliminate a 1 in 100,000 risk of a certain event, such as dying from a particular type of disease, then an agency will multiply the $60 payment times the number of individuals in the population (100,000), yielding a total of $6 million. If a rule is expected to save 100 lives, then the total benefits that can be expected to come from the rule would include $600 million in lives saved (100 lives times $6 million). According to a 2011 OMB guidance document, current agency practice uses a VSL ranging from "roughly $5 million to $9 million per statistical life." Office of Management and Budget, "Regulatory Impact Analysis: A Primer," August 15, 2011, p. 10. See also CRS Report R41140, How Agencies Monetize "Statistical Lives" Expected to Be Saved By Regulations, by Curtis W. Copeland. The author of that report is no longer at CRS; questions about its content may be directed to the author of this report.

[43] Executive Order 12866 §6(a)(3)(C).

[44] Office of Management and Budget, Circular A-4, "Regulatory Analysis," September 17, 2003. The circular is available at http://www.whitehouse.gov/omb/assets/regulatory_ matters_pdf/a-4.pdf.

[45] Executive Order 13563, "Improving Regulations and Regulatory Review," 76 Federal Register 3821, January 21, 2011.

[46] See Office of Management and Budget, "Regulatory Impact Analysis: A Primer," August 15, 2011, at http://www.whitehouse.gov/sites/default/files/omb/inforeg/regpol/circular-a-4_regulatory-impact-analysis-aprimer.pdf.

[47] 2014 OMB Report, pp. 1-3.

[48] For a discussion of this and other differences between the Obama, George W. Bush, and Clinton Administrations' priorities for cost-benefit analysis and OIRA review, see Art Fraas and Richard Morgenstern, "Identifying the Analytical Implications of Alternative Regulatory Philosophies," Journal of Benefit Cost Analysis, vol. 5, no. 1 (2014), pp. 137-171.

[49] See Rachel Bayefsky, "Dignity as a Value in Agency Cost-Benefit Analysis," Yale Law Journal, vol. 123, no. 6 (April 2014), pp. 1732-1782, at http://www.yalelawjournal.org/pdf/1732.Bayefsky.1782_u52fptmb.pdf; and Matthew D. Adler, "Fear Assessment: Cost-Benefit Analysis and the Pricing of Fear and Anxiety," Chicago-Kent Law Review, vol. 79, no. 3 (January 2004), pp. 977-1053, at http://scholarship.kentlaw.iit.edu/cgi/viewcontent.cgi?article=3459& context=cklawreview.

[50] 2014 OMB report, p. 23.

[51] See, for example, Office of Management and Budget, "Regulatory Impact Analysis: A Primer," August 15, 2011, p. 14.

[52] Kenneth J. Arrow, Maureen L. Cropper, George C. Eads, Robert W. Hahn, Lester B. Lave, Roger G. Noll, Paul R. Portney, Milton Russell, Richard Schmalensee, V. Kerry Smith, and Robert N. Stavins, "Is There a Role for Benefit-Cost Analysis in Environmental, Health, and Safety Regulation?" Science, April 12, 1996, vol. 272, pp. 221-222.

[53] Office of Management and Budget, Report to Congress on the Costs and Benefits of Federal Regulations, September 30, 1997, ch. 2, at https://www.whitehouse.gov/omb/inforeg_chap2.

[54] Cass R. Sunstein, "The Arithmetic of Arsenic," Georgetown Law Journal, vol. 90, no. 7 (July 2002), p. 2258.

[55] Cass R. Sunstein, "Financial Regulation and Cost-Benefit Analysis," Yale Law Journal Forum, January 22, 2015, p. 266, at http://www.yalelawjournal.org/pdf/ Sunstein PDF_4nf1d4ar.pdf.

[56] See, for example, Thomas O. McGarity, "CPR Perspective: Estimating Regulatory Costs," Center for Progressive Reform, at http://www.progressivereform.org/perspestima tingReg.cfm.

[57] See, for example, Stuart Shapiro, "How Much Is That Regulation In the Window?", The Hill, July 31, 2014, at http://thehill.com/blogs/pundits-blog/213538-how-much-is-that-regulation-in-the-window, stating that "agencies have clear motivations when it comes to making the assumptions that will determine their assessment of the cost of their regulations. They don't want a regulation to appear too costly or they risk losing political support for the regulation."

[58] Winston Harrington, Richard D. Morganstern, and Peter Nelson, "On the Accuracy of Regulatory Cost Estimates," Journal of Policy Analysis and Management, vol. 19, no. 2 (Spring 2000), pp. 297-322.

[59] Winston Harrington, Richard D. Morganstern, and Peter Nelson, "How Accurate Are Regulatory Cost Estimates?" Resources for the Future, March 5, 2010.

[60] Office of Management and Budget, Validating Regulatory Analysis: 2005 Report to Congress on the Benefits and Costs of Federal Regulations and Unfunded Mandates on State, Local, and Tribal Entities, available at https://www.whitehouse.gov/sites/default/files/omb/assets/omb/inforeg/2005_cb/final_2005_cb_report.pdf.

[61] As mentioned above, ex post estimates of costs and benefits are not frequently conducted under current rulemaking requirements or practice.

[62] Gabriel Chan, Robert Stavins, Robert Stowe, and Richard Sweeney, "The SO2 Allowance Trading System and the Clean Air Act Amendments of 1990: Reflections on Twenty Years of Policy Innovation," Cambridge, Mass.: Harvard Environmental Economics Program, January 2012, pp. 7-8, at http://www.hks.harvard.edu/m-rcbg/heep/papers/SO2-Brief_digital_final.pdf. See also Eban Goodstein, The Trade-Off Myth: Fact and Fiction about Jobs and the Environment (Washington, D.C.: Island Press, 1999), pp. 26-30.

[63] See Winston Harrington, Richard D. Morganstern, and Peter Nelson, "On the Accuracy of Regulatory Cost Estimates," Journal of Policy Analysis and Management, vol. 19, no. 2 (Spring 2000), p. 310.

[64] Agencies are generally required to accept public comments on proposed rules under the Administrative Procedure Act (5 U.S.C. §553).

[65] 2014 OMB Report, p. 9.

[66] 2014 OMB Report, p. 18.

[67] Winston Harrington, "Grading Estimates of the Benefits and Costs of Federal Regulation: A Review of Reviews," Resources for the Future Discussion Paper, September 2006.

[68] In the Crain and Crain report discussed in detail below, the authors state that "In summary, the constraints under which OMB operates yield cost estimates for only a small proportion of regulations... The measurement challenges lead us to adopt techniques in this study that facilitate reasonable approximations of regulatory costs that have been omitted in estimates by OMB and other studies" (pp. 5-6).

[69] W. Mark Crain and Nicole V. Crain, The Cost of Federal Regulation to the U.S. Economy, Manufacturing and Small Business, A Report for the National Association of Manufacturers, September 10, 2014, at http://www.nam.org/ CostofRegulation/.

[70] See, for example, Cheryl Bolen, "Study Commissioned by NAM Finds Regulations Cost $2 Trillion," BNA Daily Report for Executives, September 10, 2014.

[71] For example, earlier versions of the report written for the Small Business Administration's Office of Advocacy focused on the disproportionate cost of regulations on small businesses. The 2014 version, which was prepared for the National Association of Manufacturers, intended to fill an "information gap by quantifying the costs of regulatory compliance on firms, particularly manufacturers in the United States, and to extend some of the previous efforts to measure the aggregate regulatory costs." Crain and Crain 2014, p. 1.

[72] Thomas D. Hopkins, "Profiles in Regulatory Costs: Report to the U.S. Small Business Administration," November 1995, available at http://www.sba.gov/sites/default/files/files/ rs1995hoptot.pdf.

[73] The authors explained that "subsequent regulatory developments and the availability of new data clarify and in some cases amplify the basic 1995 findings: regulatory burdens continue to climb, and to disadvantage small businesses." W. Mark Crain and Thomas D. Hopkins, "The Impact of Regulatory Costs on Small Firms: A Report for the Office of Advocacy, U.S. Small Business Administration," 2001, available at http://www.sba.gov/ sites/default/files/files/ rs207tot.pdf.

[74] Again, the increase over the earlier estimate appeared to be primarily due to a change in methodology from the 2005 report. W. Mark Crain, "The Impact of Regulatory Costs on Small Firms," available at http://www.sba.gov/sites/default/files/files/rs264tot.pdf.

[75] Crain and Crain re-estimated the numbers for 2004—which were presented in the 2005 report—using the methodology from the 2014 study. After the methodological adjustment,

the estimate for 2005 increased by $445 billion to a total of $1.7 trillion, converted into 2009 dollars.

[76] These included the following: "The study is a top-down analysis of regulatory costs that uses certain assumptions to estimate totals. The study is not a bottom-up precise accounting of the overall cost of regulations. The overall figure of $1.75 trillion in costs is derived from a number of different assumptions and sources to create an estimate. As with almost any academic methodology, it was not intended to be considered a precise finding. The study demonstrated that small businesses bear a larger burden from regulations than large businesses. It was not intended to do more than provide an estimate of this disparity." See https://www.sba.gov/advocacy/impact-regulatory-costs-small-firms for these and other caveats about the study.

[77] CRS Report R41763, Analysis of an Estimate of the Total Costs of Federal Regulations, by Curtis W. Copeland. The author of that report is no longer at CRS; questions about its content can be directed to the author of this report, Maeve P. Carey.

[78] Specifically, GAO said that Advocacy did not retain the underlying information for the Crain and Crain study, making it "much more difficult to assess the quality of that work, including its objectivity." When GAO asked to speak with Crain and Crain to ask them "a set of questions related to the criticisms of the methodologies, data, and models used," Crain and Crain "would not speak with us, stating that they were no longer contractually obligated to respond to our requests for information." U.S. Government Accountability Office, Small Business Administration: Office of Advocacy Needs to Improve Controls over Research, Regulatory, and Workforce Planning Activities, GAO-14-525, July 2014, http://gao.gov/assets/670/665104.pdf; see especially pp. 13-16.

[79] The NAM study included other elements not discussed at length here because they were not part of the estimate of the total cost of regulation and therefore are not the focus of this report. For example, the study included a survey of NAM members given over a period of two weeks in 2014 that reported a number of finings, including, for example, (1) 88% of respondents said that federal government regulations were a challenge that affected their businesses in the prior year or that their businesses would face in the future; (2) 72% of respondents indicated that their organizations employed outside advisers to ensure that their operations comply with federal rules—most of these advisers consisted of attorneys, accountants, and consultants; and (3) 48% of manufacturing firms incurred operations and maintenance expenses for capital equipment and other tangible items purchased to comply with federal government requirements during the 12 months prior to the survey.

[80] As previously described, the remaining $580 billion in the Crain and Crain estimate is due to the remaining three categories—environmental, occupational safety and health and homeland security, and tax compliance regulation. Because they use the bottom-up approach to estimate each of these types of regulation, they are not discussed in this report. First, Crain and Crain arrive at a total estimate of the cost of environmental regulations using two sources: the OMB annual report to Congress on the costs and benefits of regulations, and a study from 1991 by Hahn and Hird that provides an estimate of the total costs of environmental regulations prior to 1988. See Robert W. Hahn and John A. Hird, "The Costs and Benefits of Regulation: Review and Synthesis," Yale Journal on Regulation, vol. 8, no. 1 (Winter 1991), pp. 233-278. Using these measures, they arrived at a total of $330 billion for environmental regulations. Second, to measure the occupational safety and health and homeland security regulations, they added the regulations promulgated by the Department of Homeland Security and the Occupational Safety and Health Administration (OSHA) in the Department of Labor, plus some additional calculations to measure and

include the effects of passenger delays tied to Transportation Security Administration screening. Using these measures and calculations, they arrived at a total of $92 billion for occupational safety and health and homeland security regulations. Third, Crain and Crain measure the cost of compliance with the federal tax code. To do so, they relied on the number of hours required to comply with tax requirements provided by the Internal Revenue Service. They multiplied that number of hours times an hourly wage rate of individuals who would be preparing the tax paperwork—accountants and auditors for individuals and human resources professionals for businesses. Using this method, they arrived at a total estimate of $159 billion for tax compliance. It is not exactly clear what the calculations for these figures were, because Crain and Crain did not appear to provide in their report the calculations or the hourly wages for these types of professionals.

[81] Crain and Crain 2014, p. 28.

[82] Klaus Schwab, World Economic Forum, The Global Competitiveness Report 2013-2014, Full Data Edition, Geneva, 2013, at http://reports.weforum.org/the-global-competitiveness-report-2013-2014/.

[83] According to Crain and Crain, not all three variables had observations for every year in their sample. For the years available, they used the average of the three components that were available.

[84] Crain and Crain 2014, p. 32.

[85] Each of these independent variables was lagged by one year. Crain and Crain also included tax revenues as a share of GDP squared to allow for a nonlinear effect of tax policy. This choice of independent variables was different from previous models they used, though they do not make clear why they chose different variables this time.

[86] Crain and Crain 2014, p. 33. This value appears to be adjusted to 2014 dollars.

[87] Crain and Crain do not explain why they added the cost of import restrictions. It appears they may have added it because they did not believe it would be captured in their measure of economic regulation.

[88] Rebecca Strauss, Quality Control: Federal Regulation Policy, Council on Foreign Relations, Renewing American Progress Report and Scorecard, New York, NY, March 2015, http://www.cfr.org/corporate-regulation/quality-controlfederal-regulation-policy/p36110?cid=oth-partner_site-Reg_Blog-Renewing_America_Regulation_Policy-031015; and CRS Report R43056, Counting Regulations: An Overview of Rulemaking, Types of Federal Regulations, and Pages in the Federal Register, by Maeve P. Carey.

[89] Quality Control: Federal Regulation Policy, p. 3.

[90] For a more complete discussion of how Crain and Crain constructed this variable, see Appendix C of the 2014 report.

[91] Crain and Crain 2014, p. 28.

[92] Furthermore, an incorrectly measured variable may cause some of the other estimates to be biased as well.

[93] M. A. Thomas, "What Do the Worldwide Governance Indicators Measure?" European Journal of Development Research, vol. 22 (2010), p. 37, stating that "A proposed measure of a construct, an inherently abstract concept like the 'rule of law', is like a proxy measure in that it is a hypothesis about measurement. The hypothesis is that the proposed measure correctly measures the construct. Like proposed proxy measures, not all proposed measurements of constructs are equally valid."

[94] The WGI were part of the 2010 Crain and Crain study, and, although they used a different measure in 2014, are similar in construct to the 2014 measure described above. M. A.

Thomas, “What Do the Worldwide Governance Indicators Measure?” European Journal of Development Research, vol. 22 (2010), p. 47.

[95] M. A. Thomas, “What Do the Worldwide Governance Indicators Measure?” European Journal of Development Research, vol. 22 (2010), p. 51.

[96] For a summary of Kraay’s comments, see CRS Report R41763, Analysis of an Estimate of the Total Costs of Federal Regulations, by Curtis W. Copeland.

[97] Crain and Crain did not explain why they used this different index as their main indicator in the 2014 study. They did, however, use the World Bank measurement that they had used in 2010 as an alternative proxy for the amount of regulation. The conclusions they reached with this alternative measurement were similar; see p. 71.

[98] M. A. Thomas, “What Do the Worldwide Governance Indicators Measure?” European Journal of Development Research, vol. 22 (2010), p. 36. Referenced articles include Joseph P. Forgas, “Images of Crime: A Multidimensional Analysis of Individual Differences in Crime Perception,” International Journal of Psychology, vol. 15, no. 1 (1980), pp. 287-299; Christian Pfeiffer, Michael Windzio, and Matthias Kleimann, “Media Use and its Impacts on Crime Perception, Sentencing Attitudes and Crime Policy,” European Journal of Criminology, vol. 2, no. 3 (July 2005), pp. 259-285; Benjamin A. Olken, “Corruption Perceptions vs. Corruption Reality,” NBER Working Paper No. 12428, 2006; Mitchell A. Seligson, “The Measurement and Impact of Corruption Victimization: Survey Evidence from Latin America,” World Development, vol. 34, no. 2 (2006), pp. 381-404; and Steven Van de Walle and Geert Bouckaert, “Perceptions of Productivity and Performance in Europe and the United States,” International Journal of Public Administration, vol. 30, no. 11 (2007), pp. 1123-1140.

[99] See A.H. Studenmund, Using Econometrics: A Practical Guide, 6th ed. (New York: Addison-Wesley, 2011), p. 167, stating that “the primary consideration in deciding whether an independent variable belongs in an equation is whether the variable is essential to the regression on the basis of theory.”

[100] M. A. Thomas, “What Do the Worldwide Governance Indicators Measure?” European Journal of Development Research, vol. 22 (2010), p. 41.

[101] Winston Harrington, “Grading Estimates of the Benefits and Costs of Federal Regulation: A Review of Reviews,” Resources for the Future Discussion Paper, September 2006, p. 12.

[102] A.H. Studenmund, Using Econometrics: A Practical Guide, 6th ed. (New York: Addison-Wesley, 2011), p. 207.

[103] There may be additional econometric issues with the linear regression that are beyond the scope of this report. For example, linear regression models rely on several other assumptions that are not discussed here; for a more detailed discussion of these assumptions, see Jeffrey M. Wooldridge, Introductory Econometrics: A Modern Approach, 5th ed. (South-Western - Cengage Learning, 2012).

[104] Tara M. Sinclair and Kathryn Vesey, Regulations, Jobs, and Economic Growth: An Empirical Analysis, George Washington University Regulatory Studies Center, Working Paper, Washington, DC, March 2012, p. 27, http://regulatorystudies.columbian.gwu.edu/files/downloads/032212_sinclair_vesey_reg_jobs_growth.pdf. That paper examined whether there was a relationship between changes in the on-budget costs of federal regulation in the United States and macroeconomic outcomes, and it concluded that “we found basically no evidence that the regulators’ budget has anything other than a zero effect on GDP and employment.”

[105] Stuart Shapiro and Debra Borie-Holtz, The Politics of Regulatory Reform (New York: Taylor & Francis, 2013), pp. 65-66.

[106] The R-squared in the table for "within" the countries in their sample is .01, meaning that their model is not a very good fit to explain the changes within countries over that period.

[107] Crain and Crain included dummy variables for two years, 2008 and 2009, but did not explain why.

[108] The Crain and Crain data appear to have other issues related to sample size as well. For example, their sample appears to be missing some observations—34 countries times eight years should yield 272 observations, but they report their number of observations in Table 3 to be 219. They do not provide an explanation for why these observations are missing.

[109] Furthermore, it is worth noting that the portion of their model that covers the non-economic regulation—$580 billion—may contain some of the same potential problems as those identified above for other bottom-up estimates.

[110] Executive Order 12291, "Federal Regulation," 46 Federal Register 13193, February 17, 1981, § 2(b). President William Clinton maintained this general principle of weighing costs against benefits when he issued his executive order on rulemaking, which replaced Executive Order 12291. Executive Order 12866 § 1(b)(6). In his executive order, President Clinton arguably took a slightly more lenient approach by changing the wording to require that the benefits to society justify the costs of the regulation, rather than outweigh. President Barack Obama continued to uphold the practice of comparing costs against benefits when he issued Executive Order 13563 in 2011, emphasizing, among other things, that agencies must "propose or adopt a regulation only upon a reasoned determination that its benefits justify its costs (recognizing that some benefits and costs are difficult to quantify)." Executive Order 13563 § 1(b).

[111] See CRS Report R41974, Cost-Benefit and Other Analysis Requirements in the Rulemaking Process, coordinated by Maeve P. Carey, and CRS Report RL32240, The Federal Rulemaking Process: An Overview, coordinated by Maeve P. Carey, and Eric A. Posner, "Controlling Agencies with Cost-Benefit Analysis: A Positive Political Theory Perspective," University of Chicago Law Review, vol. 68, no. 4 (Fall 2001), pp. 1137-1199, describing the "entrenchment of cost-benefit analysis in American government" in recent decades (pp. 1139-1140).

[112] A government-wide retrospective review is currently required under the Obama Administration, and similar reviews have been required by previous administrations. It is unclear, however, the extent to which agencies re-examine or recalculate their ex ante cost-benefit estimates. For more information on the current retrospective review initiative under the Obama Administration, see Joseph E. Aldy, Learning from Experience: An Assessment of the Retrospective Reviews of Agency Rules and the Evidence for Improving the Design and Implementation of Regulatory Policy, report prepared for the consideration of the Administrative Conference of the United States, November 17, 2014, at http://www.hks.harvard.edu/fs/jaldy/img/aldy_retrospective.pdf.

[113] Winston Harrington, Richard D. Morganstern, and Peter Nelson, "On the Accuracy of Regulatory Cost Estimates," Journal of Policy Analysis and Management, vol. 19, no. 2 (Spring 2000), p. 298.

In: Federal Regulations
Editor: Jamie P. Davidson

ISBN: 978-1-63485-312-5

Chapter 2

COUNTING REGULATIONS: AN OVERVIEW OF RULEMAKING, TYPES OF FEDERAL REGULATIONS, AND PAGES IN THE *FEDERAL REGISTER*[*]

Maeve P. Carey

SUMMARY

Federal rulemaking is an important mechanism through which the federal government implements policy. Federal agencies issue regulations pursuant to statutory authority granted by Congress. Therefore, Congress may have an interest in performing oversight of those regulations, and measuring federal regulatory activity can be a useful way for Congress to conduct that oversight. The number of federal rules issued annually and the total number of pages in the *Federal Register* are often referred to as measures of the total federal regulatory burden.

Certain methods of quantifying regulatory activity, however, may provide an imperfect portrayal of the total federal rulemaking burden. For example, the number of final rules published each year is generally in the range of 2,500-4,500, according to the Office of the Federal Register. Some of those rules have a large effect on the economy, and

---

[*] This is an edited, reformatted and augmented version of a Congressional Research Service publication R43056, prepared for Members and Committees of Congress, dated July 14, 2015.

others have a significant legal and/or policy effect, even if the costs and benefits are minimal. On the other hand, many federal rules are routine in nature and impose minimal regulatory burden, if any. In addition, rules that are deregulatory in nature and those that repeal existing rules are still defined as "rules" under the Administrative Procedure Act (APA, 5 U.S.C. §§551 *et seq.*) and are therefore included in that total.

The *Federal Register* provides documentation of the government's regulatory and other actions, and some scholars, commentators, and public officials have used the total number of *Federal Register* pages each year as a measure for the total amount of regulatory activity. Because the *Federal Register* has been in print since the 1930s, the number of pages can be useful for cross-time comparisons. However, the total number of *Federal Register* pages may not be an accurate way to measure regulatory activity for several reasons. In addition to publishing proposed and final rules in the *Federal Register,* agencies publish other items that may be related to regulations, such as notices of public meetings and extensions of comment periods. The *Federal Register* also contains many other items related to non-regulatory activities, including presidential documents, notices, and corrections. In 2014, approximately 32% of the total pages in the *Federal Register* were in the "Rules and Regulations" section, the section in which final rules are published.

This report serves to inform the congressional debate over rulemaking by analyzing different ways to measure federal rulemaking activity. The report provides data on and analysis of the total number of rules issued each year, as well as information on other types of rules, such as "major" rules, "significant" rules, and "economically significant" rules. These categories have been created by various statutes and executive orders containing requirements that may be triggered if a regulation falls into one of the categories. When available, data are provided on each type of rule. Finally, the report provides data on the number of pages and documents in the *Federal Register* each year and analyzes the content of the *Federal Register*.

INTRODUCTION

Federal rulemaking is an important mechanism through which the federal government implements policy. Federal agencies issue regulations pursuant to statutory authority granted by Congress.[1] Therefore, Congress may have an interest in performing oversight of those regulations, and measuring federal regulatory activity can be a useful way for Congress to conduct that oversight. The number of federal rules issued annually and the total number of pages in the *Federal Register* are often referred to as measures of the total federal regulatory burden.

Certain methods of quantifying regulatory activity, however, may provide an imperfect portrayal of the total federal rulemaking burden. For example, the number of final rules published each year is generally in the range of 2,500-4,500, according to the Office of the Federal Register. While some of those rules may have substantial economic, legal, or policy effects, many of them are routine in nature and impose minimal regulatory burden, if any.

The *Federal Register* provides documentation of the government's regulatory and other actions, and some scholars, commentators, and public officials have used the total number of *Federal Register* pages each year as a measure for the total amount of regulatory activity. Because the *Federal Register* has been in print since the 1930s, the number of pages can be useful for cross-time comparisons. However, the total number of *Federal Register* pages may not be an accurate way to measure regulatory activity for several reasons. For example, the *Federal Register* contains many other items, not all of which are related to regulations.

This report serves to inform the congressional debate over rulemaking by analyzing different ways to measure federal rulemaking activity. The report begins with a brief overview of how agencies issue rules, identifying the most significant statutory requirements, executive orders, and guidance documents that comprise the rulemaking process. The report then provides data on and analysis of the total number of rules issued each year, as well as information on other types of rules, such as "major" rules, "significant" rules, and "economically significant" rules.[2] These categories have been created by various statutes and executive orders containing requirements that may be triggered if a regulation falls into one of the categories. For example, if a rule is designated "economically significant" under Executive Order (E.O.) 12866, the issuing agency is generally required to perform a cost-benefit analysis and submit the rule for review to OMB's Office of Information and Regulatory Affairs (OIRA).[3] When available, data are provided on each type of rule.

Finally, the report presents data on the number of pages and documents in the *Federal Register* each year and analyzes the content of the *Federal Register*.

BRIEF OVERVIEW OF FEDERAL RULEMAKING

When Congress enacts legislation, it frequently delegates rulemaking authority to federal agencies. Regulations issued by agencies are often the means through which specific requirements are then established. Regulations must be issued pursuant to statutory authority, and the process under which agencies issue regulations is governed by numerous statutory requirements and executive orders. In addition, OMB has issued guidance to agencies detailing how some of those requirements should be met. This section of the report briefly describes the significant statutory and executive requirements and guidance documents.

Statutory Requirements

The most significant statute governing the rulemaking process is the Administrative Procedure Act of 1946 (APA).[4] The APA defines a *rule* as "the whole or part of an agency statement of general or particular applicability and future effect designed to implement, interpret, or prescribe law or policy."[5] The APA established standards for the issuance of rules using formal rulemaking and informal rulemaking procedures.[6] Informal rulemaking, also known as "notice and comment" rulemaking or "Section 553" rulemaking, is the most common type of rulemaking.

When issuing rules under the APA, agencies are generally required to publish a notice of proposed rulemaking (NPRM) in the *Federal Register*, take comments on the NPRM, publish a final rule in the *Federal Register*, and provide for at least a 30-day waiting period before the rule can become effective.[7] The APA specifically authorizes any federal agency to dispense with its requirements for notice and comment if the agency for good cause finds that the use of traditional procedures would be "impracticable, unnecessary, or contrary to the public interest."[8] The APA also provides a good cause exception for the 30-day waiting period between the publication of a final rule and its effective date.[9]

While the APA's notice and comment procedures comprise the general structure of the rulemaking process, a number of other statutory requirements have been added to the process in the decades since enactment of the APA.

- The *Paperwork Reduction Act* (PRA), originally enacted in 1980, established a process under which agencies have to consider the paperwork burden associated with regulatory and other actions.[10] Under the PRA, agencies generally must receive approval from OIRA for information collections from 10 or more nonfederal "persons."[11]

- The *Regulatory Flexibility Act* (RFA), also originally enacted in 1980, requires regulatory flexibility analyses for proposed and final rules that will have a "significant economic impact on a substantial number of small entities" (SEISNSE).[12] Other provisions of the RFA require that certain agencies convene advocacy review panels for rules that may have a SEISNSE to solicit feedback from affected entities and that agencies reexamine rules with a SEISNSE to determine whether any changes to or repeal of the rules may be necessary.[13]
- Title II of the *Unfunded Mandates Reform Act* (UMRA) of 1995 added requirements for agencies (other than independent regulatory agencies) to analyze costs resulting from regulations containing federal mandates upon state, local, and tribal governments and the private sector.[14] The analysis requirement in UMRA is triggered when a rule "may result in the expenditure by State, local, and tribal governments, in the aggregate, or by the private sector, of $100,000,000 or more (adjusted annually for inflation) in any 1 year."[15]
- The *Congressional Review Act* (CRA), enacted in 1996, established a mechanism through which Congress could overturn federal regulations by enacting of a joint resolution of disapproval.[16] The CRA also requires that "major" rules (e.g., those that have a $100 million effect on the economy) have a delayed effective date of at least 60 days, and that agencies submit their rules to both houses of Congress and the Government Accountability Office (GAO) before the rules can take effect. Since it was enacted, the CRA has been used one time to overturn a rule.[17]

Executive Branch Requirements and Guidance

In addition to the current statutory requirements for the rulemaking process, Presidents also have issued executive orders and OMB has issued guidance providing requirements and guidelines for agencies to follow when issuing rules.

- *E.O. 12866*, issued by President William Clinton in 1993, calls for OIRA to review "significant" regulatory actions at both the proposed and final rule stage.[18] It also requires agencies to assess potential costs and benefits for "significant" rules, and, for those deemed as "economically significant" regulatory actions, agencies are required to perform a cost-benefit analysis and assess the costs and benefits of "reasonably feasible alternatives" to the planned rule.[19] Furthermore, under E.O. 12866, agencies generally must "propose or adopt a regulation only upon a reasoned determination that the benefits" of the rule "justify its costs."[20] E.O. 12866's requirements for OIRA review and cost-benefit analysis do not apply to independent regulatory agencies.
- To provide guidance to agencies on what to include and consider in their cost-benefit analyses of rules, OMB issued *OMB Circular A-4*, a document that describes "best practices" for agencies' regulatory impact analyses.[21] OMB, under President George W. Bush, also provided guidelines for agencies to follow when issuing guidance documents.[22]
- President Barack Obama has issued several executive orders on rulemaking, and his Administration has issued a number of guidance documents for agencies on how best to issue rules. Most importantly, *E.O. 13563* reaffirmed many of the principles of E.O. 12866 and instructed agencies to conduct a retrospective review of their regulations.[23] Following the issuance of E.O. 13563, President Obama issued *E.O. 13579*, requesting that independent regulatory agencies also participate in the retrospective reviews.

NUMBER OF FINAL RULES PUBLISHED IN RECENT YEARS

Table 1 presents the approximate number of rules by year since 1976, the first year for which the Office of the Federal Register has data available.[24] The number provided in the table for each year is the number of documents published in the final rules section of the *Federal Register*.[25]

Table 1. Final Rule Documents Published in the *Federal Register*, 1976-2013

Year	Final Rule Documents Published in the *Federal Register*
1976	7,401
1977	7,031
1978	7,001
1979	7,611
1980	7,745
1981	6,481
1982	6,288
1983	6,049
1984	5,154
1985	4,843
1986	4,589
1987	4,581
1988	4,697
1989	4,714
1990	4,334
1991	4,416
1992	4,155
1993	4,369
1994	4,867
1995	4,713
1996	4,937
1997	4,584
1998	4,899
1999	4,684
2000	4,313
2001	4,132
2002	4,167
2003	4,148
2004	4,101
2005	3,943
2006	3,718
2007	3,595
2008	3,830
2009	3,503
2010	3,573
2011	3,807
2012	3,708

Table 1. (Continued)

Year	Final Rule Documents Published in the *Federal Register*
2013	3,659
2014	3,554

Source: Office of the Federal Register, Federal Register & CFR Publications Statistics, at https://www.federalregister.gov/uploads/2015/05/OFR-STATISTICS-CHARTS-ALL1-1-1-2014.pdf.

Although the number of regulations issued each year is generally in the thousands, many of those regulations deal with routine matters. For example, a rule issued on April 2, 2013, by the U.S. Coast Guard provided notice of a "temporary deviation from the operating schedule that governs the Third Street Drawbridge across the China Basin, mile 0.0, at San Francisco, CA. The deviation is necessary to allow the public to cross the bridge to participate in the scheduled CycleSF, a community event."[26] Because the change is considered a rule but only has a temporary effect, it does not make any changes to the *Code of Federal Regulations* (CFR), which is the comprehensive codification of permanent rules and regulations. Captured under the definition of a rulemaking in the APA, such items are published in the "Rules and Regulations" section of the *Federal Register*.

The number of regulations issued each year includes both new regulations as well as deregulatory actions. Under the APA, a "rulemaking" is defined as "the agency process for formulating, amending, or repealing a rule," which means that agencies must undertake a regulatory action whenever they are issuing a new rule, changing an existing rule, or eliminating a rule.[27] Therefore, not all of the regulations counted in the table above are necessarily new regulatory actions issued by agencies. Some of them could be minor amendments, including technical corrections without substantive change, or they could even include regulatory actions in which agencies are getting rid of regulations or attempting to make regulations less burdensome on the public.

"Major" Rules

As mentioned above, the CRA was enacted in 1996 and established procedures for the congressional review of agency regulations. Under the CRA, each federal agency is required to send its covered final rules to GAO and to both houses of Congress before the rules can take effect. Section 804(2) of the CRA also created a category of rules called "major" rules, which are those that the Office of Information and Regulatory Affairs Administrator determines has resulted in or is likely to result in

(A) an annual effect on the economy of $100,000,000 or more;
(B) a major increase in costs or prices for consumers, individual industries, Federal, State, or local government agencies, or geographic regions; or
(C) significant adverse effects on competition, employment, investment, productivity, innovation, or on the ability of United States-based enterprises to compete with foreign-based enterprises in domestic and export markets. The term does not include any rule promulgated under the Telecommunications Act of 1996 and the amendments made by that Act.[28]

The CRA contains two requirements for major rules. First, agencies are generally required to delay the effective dates of "major" rules until 60 days after the rule is submitted to Congress or published in the *Federal Register*, whichever is later. Second, the Comptroller General must provide a report on each major rule to the appropriate congressional committees of jurisdiction within 15 days of when a rule is submitted or published. The report must include a summary of the agency's compliance with various rulemaking requirements (such as regulatory impact analyses that agencies may be required to perform while undergoing a rulemaking action). These reports are posted on GAO's website.[29]

Table 2 presents the total number of major rules published during each calendar year since 1997, as reported by GAO.[30] Rules in the GAO database are those that have been submitted to GAO under the CRA (5 U.S.C. §801(a)(1)(A)(i)). Data begin in 1997 because the CRA was enacted in 1996, making 1997 the first full year for which data are available.

A 2011 CRS report examined the 100 major rules published in 2010 and concluded that rules are determined to be "major" for a variety of reasons, not just due to compliance costs.[31] For example, 37 of the rules appeared to be major because they involved transfers of funds from one party to another, most commonly the transfer of federal funds through programs such as grants, Medicare or Medicaid funds, special pay for members of the military, and crop subsidy payments.

Table 2. Total Number of "Major" Final Rules Published, 1997-2014

Calendar Year	Number of "Major" Final Rules
1997	61
1998	76
1999	51
2000	77
2001	70
2002	51
2003	50
2004	66
2005	56
2006	56
2007	61
2008	95
2009	84
2010	100
2011	80
2012	68
2013	80
2014	80

Source: Government Accountability Office's Federal Rules http://www.gao.gov/legal/ congressional-review-act/ about; accessed on July 8, 2015. Data provided are the numbers of major rules published each year in the Federal Register and submitted to GAO under Section 801 of the Congressional Review Act, which requires that agencies submit their rules to GAO and to both houses of Congress before they can take effect (5 U.S.C. §§801-808).

Ten other rules appeared to be major because they prompted consumer spending or because they established fees for the reimbursement of particular federal functions (e.g., issuance of passports and oversight of the nuclear power industry). Thirty-nine rules appeared to be major because they were expected to result in at least $100 million in annual benefits, costs, or both.

"Significant" Rules

The definition of a "significant" rule, found in E.O. 12866, is a rule that is likely to

1) Have an annual effect on the economy of $100 million or more or adversely affect in a material way the economy, a sector of the economy, productivity, competition, jobs, the environment, public health or safety, or State, local, or tribal governments or communities;
2) Create a serious inconsistency or otherwise interfere with an action taken or planned by another agency;
3) Materially alter the budgetary impact of entitlements, grants, user fees, or loan programs or the rights and obligations of recipients thereof; or
4) Raise novel legal or policy issues arising out of legal mandates, the President's priorities, or the principles set forth in this Executive order.[32]

Under E.O. 12866, agencies (other than independent regulatory agencies) are required to submit rules to OIRA for centralized review that are identified by agencies or determined by OIRA to be "significant." The agency must provide specific information to OIRA, including the text of the action; a detailed description of the need for the action; an explanation of how the action will meet that need; an assessment of the potential costs and benefits of the regulatory action; and an assessment of how the regulation "promotes the President's priorities and avoids undue interference with State, local, and tribal governments."[33]

While the number of major rules is accessible on GAO's Federal Rules Database, the number of significant rules issued each year is not readily available. No requirement currently exists for agencies or other entities to keep track of how many significant rules are issued each year. However, data are available for the number of reviews at OIRA each year, because OIRA logs on its website each rule it receives for review under E.O. 12866.[34] The number of "significant" rules reviewed each year is not the same as the number of "significant" rules issued each year—for example, a rule could be reviewed at OIRA late in one calendar year but not actually issued until the next calendar year. In addition, because OIRA reviews proposed and final rules, the total number of reviews is much higher than final rules issued each year. However, the number of reviews at OIRA each year may give some idea of annual regulatory activity.[35]

Table 3 lists the total number of reviews at OIRA annually from 1994-2013, including prerules, proposed rules, interim final rules, final rules, and notices.[36] Data begin in calendar year 1994 because E.O. 12866 was issued near the end of 1993.

Table 3. Total Number of Reviews at OIRA, 1994-2014

Calendar Year	Prerule Reviews	Proposed Rule Reviews	Interim Final Rule Reviews	Final Rule Reviews[a]	Notice Reviews	Total Reviews
1994	16	317	68	302	128	831
1995	8	225	64	270	53	620
1996	28	160	56	232	31	507
1997	20	196	64	174	51	505
1998	15	192	58	182	40	487
1999	19	247	71	214	36	587
2000	13	210	66	253	40	582
2001	9	274	95	285	37	700
2002	23	261	81	249	55	669
2003	23	232	92	309	59	715
2004	26	237	64	241	58	626
2005	18	221	66	247	59	611
2006	12	229	43	270	46	600
2007	22	248	44	250	25	589
2008	17	276	39	313	28	673
2009	28	214	67	237	49	595
2010	36	261	84	232	77	690
2011	24	317	76	262	61	740
2012	12	144	33	195	40	424
2013	11	177	33	160	37	418
2014	17	201	43	145	46	452

Source: The Office of Information and Regulatory Affairs's website, http://www.reginfo.gov/public/do/ eoCountsSearch; data were retrieved on July 8, 2015.

Note: The number of "significant" rules reviewed by OIRA in each year is not the same as the number of "significant" rules issued in each year. Rules are reviewed at OIRA pursuant to E.O. 12866, issued by President.

Clinton in September 1993. During the review process, OIRA examines the content of the rule; the cost-benefit analysis conducted by the agency, if any; and whether the rule is consistent with the President's priorities.

[a] The numbers in the column entitled "Final Rules Reviewed" include those rules categorized on OIRA's website as "Final Rule No Material Change," which is what agencies use to indicate to OIRA that the rule has been submitted previously under a separate action (as a proposed rule, for example) but has not had any changes since the previous submission.

"ECONOMICALLY SIGNIFICANT" RULES

"Economically significant" rules are those rules that fall into category (1) of "significant" rules, or those that may

> (1) Have an annual effect on the economy of $100 million or more or adversely affect in a material way the economy, a sector of the economy, productivity, competition, jobs, the environment, public health or safety, or State, local, or tribal governments or communities.

For rules that are considered "economically significant," agencies are required to complete a detailed cost-benefit analysis under Section 6(a)(3)(C) of E.O. 12866.[37]

Although the definition of an "economically significant" rule is very similar to the definition of a major rule, the definition of a major rule is a bit broader. Both definitions have a similar $100 million threshold, but the definition of major rule also includes other categories (see section entitled ""Major" Rules" above). As stated in OMB's guidance on implementing the Congressional Review Act,

> the main difference is that some additional rules may be captured by the CRA definition that are not considered "economically significant" under E.O. 12866, notably those rules that would have a significant adverse effect on the ability of United States-based enterprises to compete with foreign-based enterprises in domestic and export markets.[38]

Table 4 lists the total number of "economically significant" reviews and non-"economically significant" reviews by OIRA each calendar year from 1994-2013.[39]

The table refers to reviews, not just rules, because OIRA also reviews some agency guidance documents. In some cases, agencies may submit a single rule to OIRA for review more than one time in a year.

Finally, *Table 5* lists the average review times for "economically significant" and non-"economically significant" reviews from 1994-2013. Under E.O. 12866, OIRA has the responsibility to meet certain timelines for review of regulatory actions. For notices of inquiry, advanced notices of proposed rulemaking, or other "preliminary" regulatory actions, OIRA must respond to the agency within 10 working days.[40]

Table 4. Total Number of "Economically Significant" and Non-"Economically Significant" Reviews at OIRA, 1994-2014

Calendar Year	"Economically Significant" Reviews	Non-"Economically Significant" Reviews	Total Reviews
1994	134	697	831
1995	74	546	620
1996	74	433	507
1997	81	424	505
1998	73	414	487
1999	86	501	587
2000	92	490	582
2001	111	589	700
2002	100	569	669
2003	101	614	715
2004	85	541	626
2005	82	529	611
2006	71	529	600
2007	85	504	589
2008	135	538	673
2009	125	470	595
2010	138	552	690
2011	117	623	740
2012	83	341	424
2013	105	313	418
2014	114	338	452

Source: The Office of Information and Regulatory Affairs's website, http://www.reginfo.gov/public/do/ eoCountsSearch; data were retrieved on July 8, 2014.

Note: The number of "economically significant" rules reviewed by OIRA in each year is not the same as the number of "economically significant" rules issued in each year. Rules are reviewed at OIRA pursuant to E.O. 12866, issued by President Clinton in September 1993. During the review process, OIRA examines the content of the rule, the cost-benefit analysis conducted by the agency, and whether the rule is consistent with the President's priorities.

For other regulatory actions such as proposed and final rules, OIRA has 90 calendar days in which to review rules.[41] However, there are no consequences in the order if OIRA fails to meet the deadline for review.

Table 5. Average Number of Days for "Economically Significant" and Non-"Economically Significant" Reviews, 1994-2014

Calendar Year	Average Number of Days for "Economically Significant" Reviews	Average Number of Days for Non-"Economically Significant" Reviews	Average Number of Days for Review of All Items
1994	33	30	31
1995	41	35	35
1996	39	42	42
1997	47	54	53
1998	33	50	48
1999	51	53	53
2000	60	62	62
2001	46	60	58
2002	44	46	46
2003	42	50	49
2004	35	55	53
2005	39	59	57
2006	34	59	56
2007	49	64	61
2008	53	63	61
2009	33	40	39
2010	48	51	51
2011	51	60	58
2012	69	81	79
2013	120	143	137
2014	106	134	127

Source: The Office of Information and Regulatory Affairs's website; http://www.reginfo.gov/public/do/ eoCountsSearch, data were retrieved on July 8, 2015.

In every year since 1996, the average time to review "economically significant" rules has been shorter than for non-"economically significant" rules. In 2014, OIRA completed reviews for the non-"economically significant" rules roughly one month slower. One possible explanation for this trend is that "economically significant" rules might be of higher salience and political importance, therefore warranting higher priority from OIRA. Another potential reason is that OIRA frequently engages in informal reviews, collaborating with the regulatory agency in advance of the official receipt of the rule. As a result, much of the work that goes into reviewing economically significant rules may take place in advance.[42]

RULES ISSUED WITHOUT NOTICE AND COMMENT UNDER "GOOD CAUSE"

As described above, under the APA, agencies are generally required to undergo some basic steps when issuing a rule. Those steps include the publication of a proposed rule in the *Federal Register*; the opportunity for interested persons to submit comments on the proposed rule; publication of a final rule that includes a "concise general statement" of the "basis and purpose" of the rule; and at least a 30-day waiting period before the rule can take effect.[43]

The APA allows for an exception to two of these requirements if an agency has "good cause": the agency can issue a rule without notice and comment,[44] or it can waive the 30-day waiting period before the rule can take effect.[45] The agency must give supporting reasons for invoking the good cause exception, and its use of good cause is subject to judicial review.[46] Proper use of the good cause exception must reflect that following the typical notice-and-comment procedures are "impracticable, unnecessary, or contrary to the public interest."

"Interim Final" Rules

One use of the good cause exception allows agencies to issue "interim final" rules. When issuing an interim final rule, an agency invokes good cause, issues a rule, and then holds a post-promulgation comment period. If the agency is persuaded by any of the comments and so chooses, the rule can be amended in light of those comments.

"Direct Final" Rules

Federal agencies sometimes invoke another use of the good cause exception to engage in "direct final" rulemaking. "Direct final" rulemaking is used when an agency deems a rule to be routine or noncontroversial. Under "direct final" rulemaking, an agency will issue a final rule without prior notice and comment. The rule may take effect unless at least one adverse comment is received by the agency, in which case the agency must withdraw the rule and proceed with the normal notice and comment procedures. If no adverse comments are received, the rule will become effective.[47]

NUMBER OF PAGES AND DOCUMENTS IN THE *FEDERAL REGISTER*

Under the APA, agencies are required to publish proposed and final rules in the *Federal Register*.[48] Agencies also publish other items related to regulations in the *Federal Register*, such as notices of meetings and the extension of comment periods, as well as many other items related to non-regulatory governmental activities. Because the *Federal Register* provides documentation of the government's regulatory and other actions, some scholars, commentators, and public officials have used the total number of *Federal Register* pages each year, which has increased substantially since its creation, as a proxy measure for the total amount of regulatory activity.[49] The number of pages in the *Federal Register,* however, may not be an accurate proxy for regulatory activity or measure of regulatory burden for several reasons. This section discusses the history and content of the *Federal Register* and why it may not provide an accurate measure of regulatory activity.

The Federal Register Act

The Federal Register Act created the *Federal Register* in 1935 as a result of the increasing number of administrative actions, laws, and regulations associated with the New Deal. During the New Deal, the role of federal agencies changed substantially—as one scholar noted, the federal government was entering new realms of public policy as a result of laws passed under the New Deal, such as agriculture, assistance for the aged and disadvantaged, housing and home ownership, and banking and securities.[50] Many statutes that Congress passed granted rulemaking authority to these new federal agencies. To create a centralized mechanism for documenting the increasing number of rules and administrative actions, Congress created the *Federal Register*. Since the 1930s, the *Federal Register* has been the vehicle for notifying the public of the federal government's actions.

The Content of the *Federal Register*

As noted above, the number of pages in the *Federal Register* may be only a rough approximation of regulatory activity each year for several reasons. First, the section of the *Federal Register* devoted to publishing final rules is relatively small, because the *Federal Register* documents other non-regulatory activities as well. For example, in 2013, approximately 33% of the total pages were in the "Rules and Regulations" section, which is where final rules are published. The other portions of the *Federal Register* are used for such items as presidential documents, proposed rules, notices, and corrections. Other than the proposed rules, these additional sections typically have little, if anything, to do with federal regulations. Over a thousand pages each year are blank pages or skips, which are designed to leave room for other materials and to maintain the integrity of the individual sections.

Second, while the *Federal Register* provides a compilation of governmental activity that occurs each year, including new regulations that are issued, many of the final rules are amending rules that have been previously issued and therefore may not accurately be considered to be *new* rules. Similarly, as mentioned above, if an agency eliminates an already existing rule, this is considered a "rulemaking" action under the APA and would be published in the rules and regulations section of the *Federal Register*, even if it is a deregulatory action.

Third, when agencies publish proposed and final rules in the *Federal Register*, they include a preamble along with the text of the rule. The preamble often includes such information as statements of the statutory authority for the rule; information and history which the agency deems to be relevant; a discussion of the comments received during the comment period; an explanation of the agency's final decision; and in some cases, information about certain analyses that may have been required during the rulemaking process. It is possible, therefore, that the actual regulatory text provided in a rule could be relatively small compared to the size of the entire rulemaking document in the *Federal Register*. For example, a rule issued on January 25, 2013, by the Department of Health and Human Services pursuant to the Affordable Care Act modifying Health Insurance Portability and Accountability Act (HIPAA) and other regulations was 137 pages in total.[51] Of the 137 pages, 121 pages comprised the preamble and 16 pages actually amended the *Code of Federal Regulations*. Much of the preamble discussed the comments received following the NPRM, as well as estimates of costs and benefits and a list of the associated information collections.

Finally, the number of pages in the *Federal Register* may also not be an accurate reflection of the amount of regulatory burden that stems from a rule. For example, a short rule could impose a very large burden on a large number of regulated entities. On the other hand, a lengthy rule could contain less burdensome requirements but greater detail and only apply to a small number of entities. Because the preamble to the rule contains detailed information about the rule itself and the agency's response to the comments it received, the number of pages of a particular rule in the *Federal Register* could be related to other factors such as a large number of comments received or an in-depth cost-benefit analysis completed by an agency.

Figure 1 documents the change in the number of pages in the *Federal Register* over time. As the data show, the number of pages has increased since publication of the *Federal Register* began.[52] The number of pages reached a peak in 1980 at 87,012 pages; decreased to 47,418 pages in 1986; then increased again and has been approximately between 65,000 and 85,000 pages for the past two decades.

Source: Office of the Federal Register, Federal Register & CFR Publications Statistics, at https://www.federalregister.gov/uploads/2015/05/Federal-Register-Pages-Published-1936-2014.pdf.

Figure 1. Number of Pages Published Annually in the Federal Register, 1937-2014.

Table 6 provides a more detailed examination of the total page count provided in *Figure 1* and provides information on the number of pages in each rulemaking section in the *Federal Register*. In addition, *Table 6* provides data on the number of rulemaking documents in each section of the *Federal Register*. Data were obtained from the Office of the Federal Register and, at the time of writing of this report, were available from 1976 through 2013.

The number of documents published in the proposed rule and final rule sections of the *Federal Register* can be useful for cross-year comparisons. However, as mentioned above, not all of the documents in each of these sections are rules, so these data may not provide a precise count of how many rules are issued each year or of the total regulatory burden each year.

Other types of documents may also be included in the proposed and final rules sections of the *Federal Register,* as mentioned above. For example, on August 6, 2012, in the final rules section, the Federal Motor Carrier Safety Administration issued a two-page "Notice of public listening sessions and extension of comment period."[53] Because this action was related to a regulation, the document was published in the final rules section, but the document itself is not a regulation.

Finally, as previous mentioned in this report, under the APA's definition of "rulemaking," an amendment or repeal of a rule is considered a rule.[54] Therefore, some of the pages and documents counted below could be reducing the burden associated with a previously issued rule by amending or repealing the rule.

Table 6. Annual Content of the Federal Register: Number of Pages and Number of Documents, 1976-2014

	Number of Pages Published in the *Federal Register*		Number of Documents Published in the *Federal Register*	
Year	Proposed Rules	Final Rules	Proposed Rules	Final Rules
1976	9,325	12,589	3,875	7,401
1977	9,620	14,572	4,188	7,031
1978	11,885	15,452	4,550	7,001
1979	18,091	19,366	5,824	7,611
1980	16,276	21,092	5,347	7,745
1981	10,433	15,300	3,862	6,481
1982	12,130	15,222	3,729	6,288
1983	12,772	16,196	3,907	6,049
1984	11,972	15,473	3,350	5,154

Year	Number of Pages Published in the *Federal Register*		Number of Documents Published in the *Federal Register*	
	Proposed Rules	Final Rules	Proposed Rules	Final Rules
1985	13,772	15,460	3,381	4,843
1986	11,816	13,904	3,185	4,589
1987	14,181	13,625	3,423	4,581
1988	13,883	16,042	3,240	4,697
1989	13,220	16,489	3,194	4,714
1990	12,692	14,179	3,041	4,334
1991	16,761	16,792	3,099	4,416
1992	15,156	15,921	3,170	4,155
1993	15,410	18,016	3,207	4,369
1994	18,183	20,385	3,372	4,867
1995	15,982	18,047	3,339	4,713
1996	15,369	21,622	3,208	4,937
1997	15,309	18,984	2,881	4,584
1998	18,256	20,029	3,042	4,899
1999	19,447	20,201	3,281	4,684
2000	17,943	24,482	2,636	4,313
2001	14,666	19,643	2,512	4,132
2002	18,640	19,233	2,638	4,167
2003	17,357	22,670	2,538	4,148
2004	19,332	22,546	2,430	4,101
2005	18,260	23,041	2,257	3,943
2006	19,794	22,347	2,346	3,718
2007	18,611	22,771	2,308	3,595
2008	18,648	26,320	2,475	3,830
2009	16,681	20,782	2,044	3,503
2010	21,844	24,914	2,439	3,573
2011	23,193	26,274	2,898	3,807
2012	20,096	24,690	2,517	3,708
2013	20,619	26,417	2,594	3,659
2014	20,731	24,861	2,383	3,554

Source: Office of the Federal Register, Federal Register & CFR Publications Statistics, at https://www.federalregister.gov/uploads/2015/05/OFR-STATISTICS-CHARTS-ALL1-1-1-2014.pdf.

End Notes

[1] The terms "rules" and "regulations" are used interchangeably in this report.

[2] Although there are various categories of federal rules discussed in this report, the categories are not mutually exclusive. A particular regulation could fit into more than one of the categories, or in some cases a regulation may not fit into any of the categories discussed here.

[3] Executive Order 12866, "Regulatory Planning and Review," 58 Federal Register 51735, October 4, 1993. To view a copy of this order, see http://www.whitehouse.gov/omb/inforeg/eo12866.pdf. "Independent regulatory agencies" are excepted from this requirement; see discussion later in this report in section on "economically significant" rules.

[4] P.L. 79-404.

[5] 5 U.S.C. §551(4).

[6] When agencies engage in formal rulemaking, the agency must hold a trial-like hearing. Presently, formal rulemaking is a rarely used process, and its requirements are only triggered when Congress explicitly states that the rulemaking proceed "on the record" 5 U.S.C. §553(c); United States v. Florida East Coast Railway, 410 U.S. 224 (1973).

[7] 5 U.S.C. §553. Certain rules are exempted from the requirements of Section 553, including rules involving "(1) a military or foreign affairs function of the United States; or (2) a matter relating to agency management or personnel or to public property, loans, grants, benefits, or contracts" (5 U.S.C. §553(a)). In addition, certain other rules are exempted from the notice and comment requirements, but are still required to publish a final rule in the Federal Register, including "interpretative rules, general statements of policy, or rules of agency organization, procedure, or practice" (5 U.S.C. §553(b)(3)(A)).

[8] 5 U.S.C. §553(b)(B). A December 2012 Government Accountability Office (GAO) report found that agencies did not publish an NPRM in about 35% of "major" rules (those with the biggest economic effect) and about 44% of non-"major" rules published from 2003 through 2010. The most common reason agencies cited was the APA's "good cause" exception. Agencies also published rules without an NPRM for other reasons, such as cases in which the statute instructed issuance of a final rule without a prior NPRM.

[9] 5 U.S.C. §553(d)(3).

[10] 44 U.S.C. §§3501-3520. For more information about requirements under the PRA, see CRS Report R40636, Paperwork Reduction Act (PRA): OMB and Agency Responsibilities and Burden Estimates, by Curtis W. Copeland and Vanessa K. Burrows. The authors of that report are no longer at CRS; questions about the report's content can be directed to the author of this report.

[11] A "person" is defined in the act as including individuals, partnerships, associations, corporations, groups, and any element of a state or local government.

[12] 5 U.S.C. §§601-612. The RFA does not apply to rules issued without an NPRM. For more information about requirements under the RFA, see CRS Report RL34355, The Regulatory Flexibility Act: Implementation Issues and Proposed Reforms, coordinated by Maeve P. Carey.

[13] 5 U.S.C. §§609-610.

[14] 2 U.S.C. §§1532-1538. Like the RFA, UMRA does not require an analysis for rules issued without an NPRM. For more information about UMRA, see CRS Report R40957, Unfunded Mandates Reform Act: History, Impact, and Issues, by Robert Jay Dilger and

Richard S. Beth, or CRS Report RS20058, Unfunded Mandates Reform Act Summarized, by Keith Bea and Richard S. Beth.

[15] 2 U.S.C. §1532(a).

[16] 5 U.S.C. §§801-808. The CRA provides for expedited consideration of such a resolution in the Senate. For an overview of the CRA, see CRS Report R43992, The Congressional Review Act: Frequently Asked Questions, by Maeve P. Carey, Alissa M. Dolan, and Christopher M. Davis. For more detailed information about the CRA's expedited procedures, see CRS Report RL31160, Disapproval of Regulations by Congress: Procedure Under the Congressional Review Act, by Richard S. Beth.

[17] In 2001, the 107th Congress disapproved a rule on ergonomics in the workplace. See U.S. Department of Labor, Occupational Safety and Health Administration, "Ergonomics Program," 65 Federal Register 68261, November 14, 2000. Many observers suggest that the threat of a presidential veto is the reason it has only been used one time; it may be rather unlikely that the President would sign a resolution disapproving a rule from his own Administration. The ergonomics rule that was overturned was issued in the final days of the Clinton Administration, and President Bush signed the disapproval resolution soon after taking office. However, other observers have suggested that although the CRA has only been used to overturn a rule one time, its existence and the potential threat of its use acts as a check on agencies while they are writing rules.

[18] Section 6 of E.O. 12866. The E.O. defines "significant" regulatory actions as those rules that may "(1) Have an annual effect on the economy of $100 million or more or adversely affect in a material way the economy, a sector of the economy, productivity, competition, jobs, the environment, public health or safety, or State, local, or tribal governments or communities; (2) Create a serious inconsistency or otherwise interfere with an action taken or planned by another agency; (3) Materially alter the budgetary impact of entitlements, grants, user fees, or loan programs or the rights and obligations of recipients thereof; or (4) Raise novel legal or policy issues arising out of legal mandates, the President's priorities, or the principles set forth in this Executive order" (§3(f)). Rules that fall into the first of these four categories are "economically significant" rules (§3(f)(1)).

[19] Section 6(a) of E.O. 12866.

[20] Section 1(b)(6) of E.O. 12866. E.O. 12866, like its predecessor orders that were issued by President Ronald Reagan (E.O. 12291 and E.O. 12498), does not apply the cost-benefit analysis or OIRA review to independent regulatory agencies such as the Federal Reserve Board and Securities and Exchange Commission. A complete list of the independent regulatory agencies that are exempted from the order is in the Paperwork Reduction Act at 44 U.S.C. §3502(5).

[21] The most recent version of OMB Circular A-4 was issued in September 2003 and can be found on the White House's website at http://www.whitehouse.gov/omb/circulars_a004_a-4/. Circular A-4 has been used by OMB and agencies since it was issued in 2003.

[22] Guidance documents are non-binding and are issued by agencies to inform the public and/or agency staff on the implementation of regulations and statutes. For guidelines on issuing guidance documents that were issued by the Bush Administration, see Memorandum from Rob Portman, Director of the Office of Management and Budget to Heads of Executive Departments and Agencies on Issuance of OMB's Final Bulletin for Agency Good Guidance Practices, January 17, 2007, http://www.whitehouse.gov/sites/default/files/omb/memoranda/fy2007/m07-07.pdf.

[23] Executive Order 13563, "Improving Regulation and Regulatory Review," 76 Federal Register 3821, January 18, 2011. For more information on additional Obama Administration regulatory reform initiatives, see http://www.whitehouse.gov/omb/inforeg_regmatters.

[24] A previous version of this report relied upon the GAO Federal Rules Database for the total number of rules published each year. However, GAO informed CRS in a telephone conversation on November 20, 2014, that in recent years, the number of rules that agencies submitted to GAO has decreased, so the numbers from 2012 and after are no longer comparable to the numbers for prior years. The decrease in the number of rules that appear in GAO's database does not appear to apply to "major" rules, which are still reported below in Table 2.

[25] Occasionally, a document will be published in the final rules section of the Federal Register that is not an actual rule itself but does relate to a final rule(s). For example, on February 1, 2012, the Coast Guard published a notice of a public meeting and a request for comments in the final rules section of the Federal Register. That particular document was not a final rule, though it related to a previously issued proposed rule. U.S. Department of Homeland Security, Coast Guard, "Security Zone; Escorted Vessels in Captain of the Port Ohio Valley Zone," 77 Federal Register 4900, February 1, 2012.

[26] U.S. Department of Homeland Security, Coast Guard, "Drawbridge Operation Regulations; China Basin, San Francisco, CA," 78 Federal Register 19585, April 2, 2013.

[27] 5 U.S.C. §551(5).

[28] 5 U.S.C. §804(2).

[29] The major rule reports are located at http://www.gao.gov/legal/congressact/majrule.html.

[30] Because the CRA was enacted in 1996, complete data are available starting in 1997. As mentioned earlier in this report, starting in 2012, agencies submitted fewer rules to GAO under the CRA, and as a result, the total number of rules included in the GAO Federal Rules Database after 2012 is not comparable to years before 2012. However, this decrease in rules submitted did not occur for "major" rules, according to GAO.

[31] CRS Report R41651, REINS Act: Number and Types of "Major Rules" in Recent Years, by Maeve P. Carey and Curtis W. Copeland.

[32] E.O. 12866, §3(f).

[33] E.O. 12866, §6(a)(3)(B).

[34] The reviews are logged on OIRA's website at http://www.reginfo.gov/public/do/eoCountsSearchInit?action=init.

[35] As discussed above, independent regulatory agencies are not subject to the requirements under E.O. 12866 for OIRA review, so the numbers provided in Table 3 do not include any rules issued by independent regulatory agencies.

[36] Prerules are rules that are in the earliest stages of rulemaking, and may include actions agencies are considering that may or may not ever become actual rules. Interim final rules are one particular use of the APA's "good cause" exception in which agencies publish rules without prior notice and comment; see section below entitled "Interim Final Rules" for more discussion. OIRA does review some agency notices, which are non-binding documents issued by agencies and are sometimes referred to as guidance documents. See Memorandum from Peter R. Orszag, Director of the Office of Management and Budget, to Heads and Acting Heads of Executive Departments and Agencies, March 4, 2009, http://www.whitehouse.gov/sites/default/files/omb/assets/memoranda_fy2009/m09-13.pdf, stating that policy and guidance documents are "subject to OIRA's review under Executive Order 12866."

[37] OMB Circular A-4, "Regulatory Analysis," September 17, 2003, http://www.whitehouse.gov/omb/assets/regulatory_matters_pdf/a-4.pdf.

[38] Memorandum from Jacob J. Lew, Director, Office of Management and Budget, to Heads of Departments, Agencies, and Independent Establishments, March 30, 1999, "Guidance for Implementing the Congressional Review Act," p. 5, at http://www.whitehouse.gov/sites/default/files/omb/assets/memoranda_2010/m99-13.pdf. For further information on the distinction between economically significant and major rules, see the Office of Management and Budget, Regulatory Impact Analysis: Frequently Asked Questions (FAQs), February 7, 2011, pp. 1-2, http://www.whitehouse.gov/sites/default/files/omb/assets/OMB/circulars/a004/a-4_FAQ.pdf.

[39] Data are provided beginning in 1994 because E.O. 12866 was issued in September 1993. Prior to 1993, the requirement was for all rules to be reviewed, not just "significant" rules. Therefore, data on the number of OIRA reviews in years prior to 1993 are not directly comparable to data after 1993.

[40] Section 6(b)(2)(A) of E.O. 12866.

[41] Section 6(b)(2)(B) of E.O. 12866. If OIRA has previously reviewed an action and there has been "no material change" in the rule or in the "facts and circumstances upon which the regulatory action is based," then OIRA must complete its review of the action within 45 days. Section 6(b)(2)(B) of E.O. 12866 establishes a possible extension of the review process. Upon the written approval of the Director of OMB, such review can be extended by 30 days. Alternatively, the agency head can request to extend the review process for an unspecified length of time.

[42] For further discussion of the informal review process at OIRA, see Curtis W. Copeland, "Length of Rule Reviews by the Office of Information and Regulatory Affairs," Administrative Conference of the United States, October 7, 2013, p. 35, at https://www.acus.gov/sites/default/files/documents/Copeland%20Report%20CIRCULATED%20to%20Committees%20on%2010-21-13.pdf.

[43] 5 U.S.C. §553.

[44] 5 U.S.C. §553(b)(3)(B).

[45] 5 U.S.C. §553(d)(3).

[46] For more information about rulemaking and judicial review, see CRS Report R41546, A Brief Overview of Rulemaking and Judicial Review, by Todd Garvey and Daniel T. Shedd.

[47] For more information on direct final rules, see Administrative Conference of the United States (ACUS) Recommendation 95-4, available at http://www.law.fsu.edu/library/admin/acus/305954.html.

[48] For more information about exceptions to the APA's notice and comment requirements, see CRS Report R41546, A Brief Overview of Rulemaking and Judicial Review, by Todd Garvey and Daniel T. Shedd.

[49] See, for example, Clyde Wayne Crews Jr., Ten Thousand Commandments: An Annual Snapshot of the Federal Regulatory State, Competitive Enterprise Institute, Washington, DC, 2012, http://cei.org/sites/default/files/Wayne%20Crews%20-%2010,000%20 Comman dments%202012_0.pdf.

[50] Cornelius M. Kerwin, Rulemaking: How Government Agencies Write Law and Make Policy, 3rd ed. (Washington, D.C.: CQ Press, 2003), pp. 9-12.

[51] Department of Health and Human Services, "Modifications to the HIPAA Privacy, Security, Enforcement, and Breach Notification Rules Under the Health Information Technology for Economic and Clinical Health Act and the Genetic Information Nondiscrimination Act; Other Modifications to the HIPAA Rules," 78 Federal Register 5566, January 25, 2013.

[52] Office of the Federal Register, Federal Register & CFR Publications Statistics, at https://www.federalregister.gov/uploads/2015/05/OFR-STATISTICS-CHARTS-ALL1-1-1-2014.pdf.

[53] Department of Transportation, Federal Motor Carrier Safety Administration, "Notice of Public Listening Sessions and Extension of Comment Period: House of Service of Drivers of Commercial Motor Vehicles; Regulatory Guidance for Oil Field Exceptions," 77 Federal Register 46640, August 6, 2012.

[54] 5 U.S.C. §551(5).

In: Federal Regulations
Editor: Jamie P. Davidson

ISBN: 978-1-63485-312-5

Chapter 3

COST-BENEFIT AND OTHER ANALYSIS REQUIREMENTS IN THE RULEMAKING PROCESS*

Maeve P. Carey

SUMMARY

Regulatory analytical requirements (e.g., cost-benefit and cost-effectiveness analysis) have been established incrementally during the last 40 to 50 years through a series of presidential and congressional initiatives. The current set of requirements includes Executive Order 12866 and Office of Management and Budget (OMB) Circular A-4, the Regulatory Flexibility Act (RFA), and the Unfunded Mandates Reform Act (UMRA). These requirements vary in terms of the agencies and rules they cover, and the types of analyses that are required. For example, a regulatory analysis under the Regulatory Flexibility Act is not required if the agency head certifies that the rule will not have a "significant economic impact on a substantial number of small entities."

The most extensive and broadly applicable of the requirements are in Executive Order 12866 and OMB Circular A-4, but they do not apply to independent regulatory agencies. The statutes that provide rulemaking authority to independent regulatory agencies often require them to "consider" regulatory costs and benefits, and they often have less explicit

* This is an edited, reformatted and augmented version of a Congressional Research Service, Publication No. R41974, dated December 9, 2014.

requirements for cost-benefit analysis, if any. An OMB report indicated that independent regulatory agencies provided some information and costs and benefits in 76 of the 118 major rules they issued from FY2003 to FY2012. Cabinet departments and other agencies estimated monetary costs and benefits for some, but not all, of their rules.

Several bills were introduced in the 113th Congress that would codify and/or expand the current requirements for cost-benefit analysis. Congress could decide to keep the existing analytical framework in place, or could enact one or more of these reform proposals. Another more comprehensive approach could be to consolidate all of the analytical requirements in one place, and perhaps expand those requirements to include more agencies or rules, or to require different types of analysis. To do so, or to simply cover independent regulatory agencies by the executive order, the President could arguably amend Executive Order 12866 and OMB Circular A-4, or Congress could enact legislation. Any such changes must be cognizant of the state of existing law and practice in this area, and the resources and data required for agencies to carry out the analyses.

INTRODUCTION

A common concern voiced by proponents of regulatory reform in recent decades has been that the costs associated with certain regulations outweigh the benefits that the regulations are intended to provide. Another, and somewhat related, view is that more intelligent regulatory policies could achieve the same social goals (e.g., cleaner environment, safer workplaces) at less cost, or could achieve more ambitious goals at the same cost.[1] To improve the quality and effectiveness of federal rules and minimize burden, regulatory reform proponents have frequently advocated greater use of a range of analytic tools during the rulemaking process, including cost-benefit analysis (sometimes referred to as benefit-cost analysis) and cost-effectiveness analysis.[2]

Cost-benefit analysis, in this context, involves the systematic identification of all of the costs and benefits associated with a forthcoming regulation, including nonquantitative and indirect costs and benefits, and how those costs and benefits are distributed across different groups in society. A proposed regulatory requirement is judged to pass the "cost-benefit test" if the sum of its anticipated benefits outweighs, or otherwise justifies, the sum of its present and future costs in present value terms. Cost-effectiveness analysis seeks to determine how a given goal can be achieved at the least cost. In contrast to cost-benefit analysis, the concern in cost-effectiveness analysis is not with weighing the merits of the goal, but with identifying and comparing the costs of alternatives to reach that goal (e.g., in terms of dollars per life saved).

The prospective (also known as *ex ante*) estimates of benefits and costs that are done before rules are issued are necessarily uncertain and heavily dependent on numerous assumptions. Particularly difficult to quantify are long-term or uncertain effects of rules where subtle interactions between various factors are often not well understood or directly measurable. Cost-benefit analysis is particularly controversial when it seeks to rationalize inherent value trade-offs and to place a value on benefits not traded in the market (e.g., health or lives).[3] Also, Congress has required cost-benefit analysis in some statutes (as discussed in detail later in this report), prohibited it in other statutes,[4] and not precluded it in still other statutes.[5] These issues notwithstanding, many economists believe that, when used carefully and with adequate data, cost-benefit analysis can be an effective tool in regulatory decision making.[6]

Although many federal agencies are currently required to prepare cost-benefit analyses and cost-effectiveness analyses for certain rules before they are published in the *Federal Register*, proposed legislation has been introduced in the 113th Congress to expand those requirements to more agencies and more types of rules, and to produce more detailed analyses. This report identifies a number of those bills, but first describes the existing requirements for cost-benefit and other types of analysis in the federal rulemaking process. It also discusses options for changing the current set of analytical requirements. The report does not, however, attempt to address issues related to the quality of the analyses that agencies develop, or whether agencies use the results of cost-benefit analyses to guide decision making.[7]

CROSS-CUTTING REGULATORY ANALYSIS REQUIREMENTS

The current set of regulatory analytical requirements has been established incrementally during the last 40 to 50 years through a series of presidential and congressional initiatives, including statutes, executive orders, circulars, and other documents. Those initiatives vary in terms of the agencies and rules they cover, and the types of analyses that are required. Most of the analytical requirements cover Cabinet departments and "independent agencies" such as the Environmental Protection Agency (EPA), but some also cover "independent regulatory agencies" such as the Securities and Exchange Commission (SEC), the Federal Communications Commission (FCC), and the Nuclear Regulatory Commission (NRC).[8]

Presidential Initiatives

Each President within the past 40 years has required some form of regulatory analysis before agencies' rules are published in the *Federal Register*. For example:

- In 1971, President Nixon required agencies to develop a summary of their regulatory proposals, a description of the alternatives that they considered, and the costs of those alternatives.[9]
- In 1974, President Ford required agencies to develop an "inflation impact statement" for each major proposed rule.[10]
- In 1978, President Carter required agencies to prepare a regulatory analysis that examined the cost-effectiveness of the alternative regulatory approaches for major rules.[11]

Current broadly applicable cost-benefit analysis requirements in the rulemaking process are primarily traceable to President Reagan's Executive Order 12291, which was issued in February 1981.[12] Under that executive order, the "covered agencies" (Cabinet departments and independent agencies, but not independent regulatory agencies) were generally required to (1) refrain from taking regulatory action "unless the potential benefits to society for the regulation outweigh the potential costs to society," (2) select regulatory objectives to maximize net benefits to society, and (3) select the regulatory alternative that involved the least net cost to society. The order also required covered agencies to prepare a "regulatory impact analysis" for each "major" rule, which was defined as any regulation likely to result in (among other things) an annual effect on the economy of $100 million. Those analyses were required to contain a description of the potential benefits and costs of the rule, a determination of the net benefits of the rule, a description of alternative approaches that could substantially achieve the regulatory goal at lower cost, and an explanation of why those approaches were not selected.

Executive Order 12866

Executive Order 12291 remained in place until September 1993, when President Clinton issued Executive Order 12866.[13] The Clinton executive order, which is still in effect, revoked the Reagan order, but established analytical principles and requirements that are similar (although not identical) to those it replaced. For example, in its "Statement of Regulatory Philosophy" in Section 1(a), Executive Order 12866 states that the "covered agencies" (again, Cabinet departments and independent agencies, but not independent regulatory agencies)[14]

> should assess all costs and benefits of available regulatory alternatives, including the alternative of not regulating. Costs and benefits shall be understood to include both quantifiable measures (to the fullest extent that these can be usefully estimated) and qualitative measures of costs and benefits that are difficult to quantify, but nevertheless essential to consider. Further, in choosing among alternative regulatory approaches, agencies should select those approaches that maximize net benefits (including potential economic, environmental, public health and safety, and other advantages; distributive impacts; and equity), unless a statute requires another regulatory approach.

Section 1(b) of Executive Order 12866 delineates certain "Principles of Regulation" that covered agencies "should adhere to" (to the extent permitted by law and where applicable). For example, the agencies are told that they should

- design their regulations "in the most cost-effective manner to achieve the regulatory objective. In doing so, each agency shall consider incentives for innovation, consistency, predictability, the costs of enforcement and compliance (to the government, regulated entities, and the public), flexibility, distributive impacts, and equity";
- assess both the costs and the benefits of their intended regulations and, "recognizing that some costs and benefits are difficult to quantify, propose or adopt a regulation only upon a reasoned determination that the benefits of the intended regulation justify its costs";[15] and
- tailor their regulations "to impose the least burden on society, including individuals, businesses of differing sizes, and other entities (including small communities and governmental entities), consistent

with obtaining the regulatory objectives, taking into account, among other things, and to the extent practicable, the costs of cumulative regulations."

The heart of the economic analysis requirements is in Section 6 of Executive Order 12866, which differentiates between "significant" and "economically significant" rules. "Significant" rules are defined as those that satisfy any of four conditions:

> (1) Have an annual effect on the economy of $100 million or more or adversely affect in a material way the economy, a sector of the economy, productivity, competition, jobs, the environment, public health or safety, or State, local, or tribal governments or communities;
>
> (2) Create a serious inconsistency or otherwise interfere with an action taken or planned by another agency; (3) Materially alter the budgetary impact of entitlements, grants, user fees, or loan programs or the rights and obligations of recipients thereof; or (4) Raise novel legal or policy issues arising out of legal mandates, the President's priorities, or the principles set forth in this Executive order.[16]

Rules fitting the first of these conditions are often referred to as "economically significant" or "major" regulatory actions.[17]

Section 6(a)(3)(B) of Executive Order 12866 states that, for each "significant" regulatory action, covered agencies are to provide to the Office of Information and Regulatory Affairs (OIRA) within the Office of Management and Budget (OMB) a general "assessment of the potential costs and benefits of the regulatory action." However, Section 6(a)(3)(C) of the executive order states that, for each "economically significant" regulatory action, agencies are to also provide to OIRA (unless prohibited by law):

> (i) An assessment, including the underlying analysis, of benefits anticipated from the regulatory action (such as, but not limited to, the promotion of the efficient functioning of the economy and private markets, the enhancement of health and safety, the protection of the natural environment, and the elimination or reduction of discrimination or bias) together with, to the extent feasible, a quantification of those benefits;
>
> (ii) An assessment, including the underlying analysis, of costs anticipated from the regulatory action (such as, but not limited to, the direct cost both to the government in administering the regulation and to

businesses and others in complying with the regulation, and any adverse effects on the efficient functioning of the economy, private markets (including productivity, employment, and competitiveness), health, safety, and the natural environment), together with, to the extent feasible, a quantification of those costs; and

(iii) An assessment, including the underlying analysis, of costs and benefits of potentially effective and reasonably feasible alternatives to the planned regulation, identified by the agencies or the public (including improving the current regulation and reasonably viable nonregulatory actions), and an explanation why the planned regulatory action is preferable to the identified potential alternatives.

In emergency situations, or when an agency is required by law to act more quickly than normal review procedures allow, the rulemaking agency is required to comply with the order's requirements "to the extent practicable."[18] Section 10 of Executive Order 12866 states that nothing in the order affects otherwise available judicial review,[19] and it goes on to say that the order "is intended only to improve the internal management of the Federal Government and does not create any right or benefit, substantive or procedural, enforceable by law or equity by a party against the United States, its agencies or instrumentalities, its officers or employees, or any other person."

OMB Circular A-4

In January 1996, OIRA published a document that described "best practices" for preparing the economic analyses called for by the executive order.[20] In essence, the best practices document said that the analysis should (1) clearly state the need for the proposed action (e.g., market failure) and make clear why federal regulation (as opposed to other methods such as state regulation or subsidies) is the appropriate solution, (2) clearly show that the agency considered the most important alternative approaches, and (3) assess the incremental costs and benefits of the proposed action. The best-practices document also stated that cost-effectiveness analysis should be used where possible to evaluate alternatives.

In September 2003, OMB and the Council of Economic Advisors finalized OMB Circular A-4 on "Regulatory Analysis," which refined and replaced the 1996 best practices document.[21] The circular states that it was "designed to assist analysts in the regulatory agencies by defining good regulatory analysis ... and standardizing the way benefits and costs of Federal regulatory actions are measured and reported."[22] It also states that a "good regulatory analysis should include the following three basic elements: (1) a statement of the need for the proposed action, (2) an examination of alternative approaches, and (3) an evaluation of the benefits and costs— quantitative and qualitative—of the proposed action and the main alternatives identified by the analysis."[23]

- With regard to need, OMB Circular A-4 states that the agency should describe the statutory or judicial directives that authorize the action, and describe the problem that it intends to address. The underlying problem can involve a market failure (e.g., a monopoly that adversely affects consumers, or inadequate information about a product) or other social purposes (e.g., to combat discrimination). The statement of need should also consider other alternatives to federal regulation, including the option of state or local regulation.
- After determining that federal regulation is needed, OMB Circular A-4 requires the agency to consider a "reasonable number" of alternative regulatory approaches available within the statutory authority provided to the agency. For example, the circular says agencies should consider different compliance dates, enforcement methods, levels of stringency, requirements based on firm size or geographic region; performance standards instead of design standards, market approaches instead of direct controls; and informational measures instead of regulation.
- With regard to analytical approaches, the circular states that agencies should use both cost-benefit analysis and cost-effectiveness analysis. When all benefits and costs can be expressed in monetary units, cost-benefit analysis can clearly indicate which approach is most efficient in terms of net benefits.[24] However, in many (and perhaps most) cases, agencies are not able to express all of the benefits or costs in monetary units. In such cases, OMB Circular A-4 states that cost-benefit analysis "is less useful, and it can even be misleading, because the calculation of net benefits in such cases does not provide a full evaluation of all relevant benefits and costs."[25] Analysts should therefore attempt to quantify benefits or costs as much as possible (e.g., tons of pollution avoided, or the number of children who will not suffer discrimination), and "exercise professional judgment" in determining whether non-quantified factors are important enough to justify consideration of the regulation.

Although some contend that certain benefits cannot be monetized (e.g., deaths or illnesses avoided),[26] agencies have developed a variety of methods of doing so, often by determining the number of "statistical lives" that the rules are expected to extend or save, and then multiplying that number by an estimated "value of a statistical life" (VSL).[27] OMB Circular A-4 notes that academic studies have identified VSLs from $1 million to $10 million, but it does not recommend that agencies use a particular VSL. In 2009, the Department of Transportation's (DOT's) VSL was $6.0 million while the Environmental Protection Agency's (EPA's) VSL was nearly $7.9 million.[28]

OMB Circular A-4 describes cost-effectiveness analysis as a way to "identify options that achieve the most effective use of the resources available without requiring monetization of all of relevant benefits or costs."[29] It allows analysts to compare a set of regulatory actions with the same primary outcome. For example, the analysis may indicate that one option costing $100 million is expected to save 50 lives (i.e., $2 million per life saved), while another option costing $200 million is expected to save 200 lives during the same period (i.e., $1 million per life saved).

The circular also discusses a variety of other economic analysis issues, including measuring costs and benefits against a baseline (i.e., the way the world would look absent the proposed regulation); discounting when benefits and costs do not occur within the same time period; and how uncertainty should be treated (e.g., ranges, probability distributions, and estimates of expected value). For particularly large rules with annual economic effects of $1 billion or more, agencies are instructed to

> present a formal quantitative analysis of the relevant uncertainties about benefits and costs. In other words, you should try to provide some estimate of the probability distribution of regulatory benefits and costs. In summarizing the probability distributions, you should provide some estimates of the central tendency (e.g., mean and median) along with any other information you think will be useful such as ranges, variances, specified low-end and high-end percentile estimates, and other characteristics of the distribution.[30]

Finally, OMB Circular A-4 provides guidance on the regulatory accounting statements that are required under the Regulatory Right-to-Know Act,[31] and summarizes analytical requirements in other statutes and executive orders.

Executive Orders 13563 and 13579

Executive Order 13563, issued by President Obama in January 2011, reiterated many of the general principles of regulation in Executive Order 12866.[32] For example, it says covered agencies (Cabinet departments and independent agencies) must (to the extent permitted by law): (1) propose or adopt a regulation only upon a reasoned determination that its benefits justify its costs, (2) tailor regulations to impost the least burden on society, and (3) select regulatory approaches that maximize net benefits. It also directs agencies to "use the best available techniques to quantify anticipated present and future benefits and costs as accurately as possible." Section 6 of the executive order requires covered agencies to develop a plan under which they would periodically review their existing significant rules. Although the executive order does not apply to independent regulatory agencies, a February 2011 memorandum from the OIRA Administrator encouraged those agencies to "give consideration to all its provisions."[33]

In July 2011, President Obama issued Executive Order 13579, "Regulation and Independent Regulatory Agencies."[34] The executive order encouraged independent regulatory agencies to comply with some of the principles in Executive Order 13563 that were directed to Cabinet departments and independent agencies (e.g., public participation, integration and innovation, flexible approaches, and science), and said independent regulatory agencies "should" develop a plan for the periodic review of their rules. In a separate memorandum issued the same day as the executive order, the President said he was doing so with "full respect for the independence of your agencies."[35] Executive Order 13579 does not, however, directly apply the cost-benefit principles in Executive Orders 12866 or 13563 to independent regulatory agencies, and does not require them to conduct any type of economic analysis before issuing their rules.

Analytical Requirements in Other Executive Orders

In addition to the broadly applicable analytical requirements in Executive Order 12866 and related guidance, several other executive orders have required covered agencies (Cabinet departments and independent agencies) to analyze their regulations for particular purposes. For example:

- Executive Order 13045 on "Protection of Children from Environmental Health Risks and Safety Risks," issued in April 1997, requires each covered agency, "to the extent permitted by law and appropriate, and consistent with the agency's mission," to "address disproportionate risks to children that result from environmental health risks or safety risks."[36] For any substantive rulemaking action that "is likely to result in" an economically significant rule that concerns "an environmental health risk or safety risk that an agency has reason to believe may disproportionately affect children," the agency must provide OIRA with "an evaluation of the environmental health or safety effects of the planned regulation on children," as well as "an explanation of why the planned regulation is preferable to other potentially and reasonably feasible alternatives considered by the agency."

- Executive Order 13132 on "Federalism," issued in August 1999, requires covered agencies to prepare a "federalism summary impact statement" whenever they issue a rule that has "significant federalism implications."[37] The assessment is to contain "a description of the extent of the agency's prior consultation with State and local officials, a summary of the nature of their concerns and the agency's position supporting the need to issue the regulation, and a statement of the extent to which the concerns of State and local officials have been met." The executive order says the consultation and impact statement requirements apply "to the extent practicable."[38]
- Executive Order 13175 on "Consultation and Coordination with Indian Tribal Governments" requires covered agencies to "have an accountable process to ensure meaningful and timely input by tribal officials in the development of regulatory policies that have tribal implications." In addition, the order states that no agency shall promulgate a regulation that has tribal implications and preempts tribal law without first consulting with tribal officials, providing OMB with a "tribal summary impact statement," and making available to OMB any written communications the tribal officials submitted to the agency.[39]
- Executive Order 13211, issued in May 2001, requires covered agencies (to the extent permitted by law) to prepare and submit to OMB a "Statement of Energy Effects" for "significant energy actions."[40] The statement, which is to be published in the proposed rule and the final rule, is to include a detailed statement of "any adverse effects on energy supply, distribution, or use" for the action, and reasonable alternatives and their effects.

None of these executive orders apply to independent regulatory agencies, and all of them give federal agencies substantial discretion to define key terms (e.g., "disproportionately affect," "significant federalism implications," and "significant energy actions") that determine the degree to which they cover agencies' rules.

Supplemental Publications

On October 28, 2010, OMB published an agency checklist for the regulatory impact analyses required by Executive Order 12866 and OMB Circular A-4.[41] It contains repeated references to provisions in the executive order and the circular, and states that nothing in the checklist "alters, adds to, or reformulates existing requirements in any way." Among other things, the checklist asks whether the agency's analysis (1) has a reasonably detailed description of the need for the regulatory action, (2) explains how the action will meet that need, (3) quantifies and monetizes the expected costs and benefits of the action to the extent feasible, (4) explains and supports a reasoned justification that the benefits of the regulatory action justify the costs, (5) assesses the potentially effective and reasonable alternatives to the action (including at least one alternative that is more stringent and one that is less stringent), and (6) explains why the planned regulatory action is preferable to those alternatives.

On February 7, 2011, OMB published a document entitled *Regulatory Impact Analysis: Frequently Asked Questions*.[42] Again, OMB said "nothing said here is meant to alter existing requirements in any way." Among other things, OMB indicated the following:

- A rule may be considered "economically significant" if it is expected to have $100 million in costs, benefits, or transfers in any one year, and rules that do not cross that threshold but could adversely affect a small sector of the economy and would threaten to create significant job loss would still be considered "economically significant."
- Agencies' regulatory impact analyses should be presented in plain language, and should include a clear executive summary of their central conclusions and an accounting statement with a table summarizing the expected costs, benefits, and transfers.
- When considering regulatory alternatives, agencies should begin by asking whether to regulate at all, and should consider deferring to regulation at the state or local level. If federal regulation is needed, agencies should consider analyzing at least three options: the

preferred option, a more stringent option, and a less stringent one. Agencies should also generally include a sensitivity analysis showing how results can vary with changes in assumptions, data, and analytical approaches.

In August 2011, OMB issued a primer to "assist agencies in developing regulatory impact analyses (RIAs), as required for economically significant rules by Executive Order 13563, Executive Order 12866, and OMB Circular A-4." The primer contains nine steps for conducting a proper regulatory impact analysis: (1) describe the need for the regulatory action; (2) define the baseline; (3) set the time horizon of analysis; (4) identify a range of regulatory alternatives; (5) identify the consequences of regulatory alternatives; (6) quantify and monetize the benefits and costs; (7) discount future benefits and costs; (8) evaluate non-quantified and non-monetized benefits and costs; and (9) characterize uncertainty in benefits, costs, and net benefits.[43]

Congressional Initiatives

Congress has also required federal agencies to analyze the effect of certain rules before they are issued. Some of the requirements are potentially applicable to a range of agencies and regulations, while other requirements are focused on particular agencies or types of rules (e.g., those affecting the environment or small businesses). In addition to the cross-cutting requirements discussed below, there are many other requirements that are tied to particular agencies and statutes. For example, Section 1102(b) of the Social Security Act (42 U.S.C. §1302(b)) requires the Department of Health and Human Services to prepare a regulatory impact analysis if a rule may have a significant impact on the operations of a substantial number of small rural hospitals.[44]

Unfunded Mandates Reform Act

The statutory provisions that most closely approximate the types of analysis required in Executive Order 12866 are in Title II of the Unfunded Mandates Reform Act (UMRA) of 1995 (2 U.S.C. §§1532-1538).[45] Before promulgating a rule containing a mandate that may result in the expenditure of $100 million or more in any one year by the private sector, or by state, local, and tribal governments in the aggregate, UMRA requires covered agencies

(Cabinet departments and independent agencies, but not independent regulatory agencies) to prepare a written statement containing (among other things) a "qualitative and quantitative assessment of the anticipated costs and benefits ... as well as the effect of the Federal mandate on health, safety, and the natural environment." The written statement is also generally required to include estimates of future compliance costs, and any disproportionate budgetary effects on particular regions, governments, or segments of the private sector, and estimates of effects on the national economy, including effects on job creation, productivity, full employment, and international competitiveness. OIRA has primary responsibility for monitoring agency compliance with Title II of UMRA, and publishes an annual report on the implementation of Title II.[46] UMRA provides for limited judicial review of agency compliance with these analytical requirements. Specifically, Section 401(a)(2)(B) states that if an agency fails to prepare the written statement required in Section 202, "a court may compel the agency to prepare such written statement."

As the Government Accountability Office (GAO, formerly the General Accounting Office) pointed out several times during the past 15 years, however, UMRA's analytical requirements do not apply to most economically significant rules, give agencies substantial discretion regarding their implementation, and do not require agencies to do much more than is already required in Executive Order 12866. For example, the requirements in Section 202 of UMRA are not triggered if the agency issues a final rule without a previous notice of proposed rulemaking. (About half of all final rules do not have a prior proposed rule.)[47] Also, UMRA does not apply unless there are "expenditures" of at least $100 million in a year (which may not be the same as "impact on the economy" or even "cost"), and does not apply to "voluntary" programs or conditions of federal financial assistance. Agencies do not have to estimate certain effects if they determine such estimates are not "reasonably feasible." In February 1998, GAO reported that, because of the way the statute was written, Title II of UMRA had little effect on agencies' rulemaking actions during its first two years of implementation.[48] In May 2004, GAO again reported that UMRA's written statement requirements did not apply to most major or economically significant final rules issued in 2001 and 2002, even though some of the rules "appeared to have potential financial impacts on affected nonfederal parties similar to those of the actions that were identified as containing mandates at or above the act's thresholds."[49] In February 2011, GAO reiterated these conclusions, noting that there are at least 14 reasons why a rule would not be considered a "mandate" under UMRA.[50]

National Environmental Policy Act

Other statutory analytical requirements have been enacted with regard to particular issues or constituencies. For example, the National Environmental Policy Act (NEPA) of 1969 (42 U.S.C. §§4321-4347) requires federal agencies to include in every recommendation or report related to "major Federal actions significantly affecting the quality of the human environment" a detailed statement on the environmental impact of the proposed action.[51] The environmental impact statement must delineate the direct, indirect, and cumulative effects of the proposed action. Agencies are also required to include in the statement (1) any adverse environmental effects that cannot be avoided should the proposal be implemented, (2) alternatives to the proposed action, (3) the relationship between local short-term uses of the environment and the maintenance and enhancement of long-term productivity, and (4) any irreversible and irretrievable commitments of resources that would be involved if the proposed action should be implemented. As discussed in a separate CRS report, just about every word in the term "major Federal actions significantly affecting the quality of the human environment" has been disputed, scrutinized, and defined by the courts.[52]

Regulatory Flexibility Act

The Regulatory Flexibility Act (RFA) of 1980 (5 U.S.C. §§601-612) requires federal agencies to assess the impact of their forthcoming regulations on "small entities," which the act defines as including small businesses, small governmental jurisdictions, and certain small not-for-profit organizations. Under the RFA, Cabinet departments and independent agencies as well as independent regulatory agencies must prepare a "regulatory flexibility analysis" at the time proposed and certain final rules are issued. The RFA requires the analysis to describe, among other things, (1) the reasons why the regulatory action is being considered; (2) the small entities to which the proposed rule will apply and, where feasible, an estimate of their number; (3) the projected reporting, recordkeeping, and other compliance requirements of the proposed rule; and (4) any significant alternatives to the rule that would accomplish the statutory objectives while minimizing the impact on small entities.[53]

However, these analytical requirements are not triggered if the head of the issuing agency certifies that the proposed rule would not have a "significant economic impact on a substantial number of small entities." The RFA does not define "significant economic impact" or "substantial number of small entities," thereby giving federal agencies substantial discretion regarding when the act's analytical requirements are initiated. Also, the RFA's analytical requirements do not apply to final rules for which the agency does not publish a proposed rule, and some agencies do not consider an RFA analysis to be required if the rule is expected to have significant positive effects on small entities.[54]

The RFA initially did not permit judicial review of agencies' actions under the act. However, amendments to the act in 1996 as part of the Small Business Regulatory Enforcement Fairness Act (SBREFA, 5 U.S.C. §601 note) permitted judicial review regarding, among other things, agencies' regulatory flexibility analyses for final rules and any certifications that their rules will not have a significant impact on small entities. As a result, a small entity that is adversely affected or aggrieved by an agency's determination that its final rule would not have a significant impact on small entities could seek judicial review of that determination within one year of the date of the final agency action. In granting relief, a court may remand the rule to the agency or defer enforcement against small entities. For more than 25 years, however, courts have ruled that agencies need not prepare regulatory flexibility analyses if the effects of a rule on an industry are indirect.[55] Therefore, for example, if a federal agency is issuing a final rule establishing a health standard that is implemented by states or other entities, the federal agency issuing the rule need not prepare a regulatory flexibility analysis even if it is clear that the implementation ultimately will have significant effect on a substantial number of small entities.[56]

GAO has examined the implementation of the RFA several times within the past 20 years, and a recurring theme in GAO's reports is a lack of clarity in the act and a resulting variability in its implementation. For example, in 1991 GAO reported that each of the four federal agencies that it reviewed had a different interpretation of key RFA provisions.[57] In 1994, GAO again reported that agencies' compliance with the RFA varied widely from one agency to another and that agencies were interpreting the statute differently.[58] In a 1999 report, GAO concluded that agencies had broad discretion to determine what the statute required.[59] In a 2000 report, GAO said that the Environmental Protection Agency (EPA) had certified more than 95% of its final rules issued in the late 1990s, and characterized EPA as having a "high threshold" for analysis (albeit within the discretion permitted in the statute).[60] In all of these reports, GAO suggested that Congress consider clarifying the act's requirements and/or give the Small Business Administration (SBA) or some other entity the responsibility to develop criteria for whether and how agencies should conduct RFA analyses.[61] In 2001, GAO testified that the promise of the RFA may never be realized until Congress or some other entity defines what a "significant economic impact" and a "substantial number of small entities" mean in a rulemaking setting.[62] However, other observers have indicated that the definitions of these terms should remain flexible because of significant differences in each agency's operating environment.[63]

Paperwork Reduction Act

Other analytical requirements pertain to certain aspects of the rulemaking process, albeit not the rules themselves. The Paperwork Reduction Act (PRA) (44 U.S.C. §§3501-3520) was originally enacted in 1980, but was subsequently amended in 1986 and again in 1995. One of the purposes of the PRA is to minimize the paperwork burden for individuals, small businesses, and others resulting from the collection of information by or for the federal government. The act generally defines a "collection of information" as the obtaining or disclosure of facts or opinions by or for an agency (Cabinet departments and independent agencies as well as independent regulatory agencies) by 10 or more nonfederal persons. Many information collections, recordkeeping requirements, and third-party disclosures are contained in or are authorized by regulations as monitoring or enforcement tools. In fact, these paperwork requirements are the essence of many agencies' regulatory provisions.[64] The PRA requires agencies to justify any collection of information from the public by establishing the need and intended use of the information, estimating the burden that the collection will impose on respondents, and showing that the collection is the least burdensome way to gather the information.

The original PRA established OIRA to provide central agency leadership and oversight of government-wide efforts to reduce unnecessary paperwork burden and improve the management of information resources. Agencies must receive OIRA approval (signified by an OMB control number displayed on the information collection) for each collection request before it is implemented, and those approvals must be renewed at least every three years. Failure to obtain OIRA approval for an active collection, or the lapse of that approval, represents a violation of the act, and triggers the PRA's public protection provision. Under that provision, no one can be penalized for failing to comply with a collection of information subject to the act if the collection does not display a valid OMB control number.[65] OIRA can disapprove any collection of information if it believes the collection is inconsistent with the requirements of the PRA. However, multi-headed independent regulatory agencies can, by majority vote of the leadership, void any OIRA disapproval of a proposed information collection.[66]

Coverage of Analytical Requirements Varies

As the above discussion indicates, the cross-cutting executive order and statutory analytical requirements vary substantially in terms of the types and amount of analysis required, and the agencies and rules that they cover:

- Executive Order 12866 and OMB Circular A-4 contain the most detailed requirements, and cover all rules with a $100 million annual "effect on the economy," but the executive order and the circular do not apply to independent regulatory agencies.
- The Unfunded Mandates Reform Act contains analytical requirements that are somewhat similar to those in Executive Order 12866, but it applies to only a small percentage of the rules that are covered by the executive order because of substantial limitations in the scope of the act's requirements (e.g., UMRA does not apply to independent regulatory agencies, or to rules that are conditions of financial assistance, rules issued without a notice of proposed rulemaking, or rules that do not require $100 million in "expenditures" in a year).
- The Regulatory Flexibility Act is broader than either the executive order or UMRA in that it covers independent regulatory agencies, but the RFA does not apply to rules issued without a notice of proposed rulemaking, or to rules that the agencies certify will not have a "significant economic impact on a substantial number of small entities." Some agencies certify that more than 90% of their rules will not have that impact, and therefore are not required to do the analysis.
- The Paperwork Reduction Act covers independent regulatory agencies, but it only covers agencies' collections of information, not the rules themselves.

Table 1 below summarizes this information, showing that the requirement with most extensive analytical requirements and broad coverage (Executive Order 12866) does not apply to independent regulatory agencies, and the requirements that do apply to independent regulatory agencies (the RFA and the PRA) are more limited in the types of analysis required.

Table 1. Depth and Coverage of Analytical Requirements Vary

Analytical Requirement	Cabinet Departments and Independent Agencies	Independent Regulatory Agencies
Extensive Analytical Requirements and Broad Rule Coverage		
Executive Order 12866 and OMB Circular A-4 Yes		No
Limited Analytical Requirements and/or Narrow Rule Coverage		
Other executive orders Yes		No
Unfunded Mandates Reform Act Yes		No
NEPA Yes		Yes
Regulatory Flexibility Act Yes		Yes
Paperwork Reduction Act Yes		Yes

Source: CRS.

Analytical Requirements Applicable to Selected Independent Regulatory Agencies

Although independent regulatory agencies are not covered by the analytical requirements in Executive Order 12866 and OMB Circular A-4, that lack of coverage may be ameliorated if the individual statutes that provide rulemaking authority to these agencies require cost-benefit or other types of economic analysis. This section of the report examines the analytical requirements in the underlying statutes for selected independent regulatory agencies.

Economic Analysis and Banking Agencies

Because of concerns regarding the implementation of the Dodd-Frank Wall Street Reform and Consumer Protection Act (P.L. 111-203, July 21, 2010), on May 4, 2011, the 10 Republican Senators on the Senate Committee on Banking, Housing, and Urban Affairs jointly requested that the offices of the inspectors general (OIGs) for five independent regulatory agencies in the banking area provide them with information about the economic analysis requirements applicable to rulemaking in those agencies.[67] The five agencies were the Board of Governors of the Federal Reserve System, the Securities and Exchange Commission (SEC), the Commodity Futures Trading Commission (CFTC), the Office of the Comptroller of the Currency (OCC) within the Department of the Treasury, and the Federal Deposit Insurance

Corporation (FDIC). The five OIGs provided written responses to the Senators in June 2011, and those responses are summarized below.

Board of Governors of the Federal Reserve System

The OIG for the Board of Governors of the Federal Reserve System said that statutes related to the board's rulemaking authority, including the Federal Reserve Act and the Bank Holding Company Act of 1956, "generally do not require economic analysis as part of the agency's rulemaking activities."[68] The OIG noted the applicability of the PRA and the RFA to the Board's rulemaking, but said they only require "narrowly tailored evaluations of the rulemaking's paperwork burden and effect on small entities, respectively."[69]

Securities and Exchange Commission

The SEC OIG report identified several statutory provisions that require the commission to analyze the impact of its rules.[70] For example, the report noted that the National Securities Market Improvement Act (15 U.S.C. §77b(b)) requires the SEC to consider whether an action "will promote efficiency, competition, and capital formation" whenever it is "engaged in rulemaking and is required to consider or determine whether an action is necessary or appropriate in the public interest." Also, Section 23(a)(2) of the Securities Exchange Act of 1934 (15 U.S.C. §78w(a)(2)) states that:

> The Commission and the Secretary of the Treasury, in making rules and regulations pursuant to any provisions of this chapter, shall consider among other matters the impact any such rule or regulation would have on competition. The Commission and the Secretary of the Treasury shall not adopt any such rule or regulation which would impose a burden on competition not necessary or appropriate in furtherance of the purposes of this chapter. The Commission and the Secretary of the Treasury shall include in the statement of basis and purpose incorporated in any rule or regulation adopted under this chapter, the reasons for the Commission's or the Secretary's determination that any burden on competition imposed by such rule or regulation is necessary or appropriate in furtherance of the purposes of this chapter.

The OIG noted that the RFA and the PRA apply to SEC rulemaking, and that Executive Order 12866 and OMB Circular A-4 do not apply. Nevertheless, the OIG said that "SEC Chairmen have made a commitment to Congress that the SEC will conduct cost-benefit or economic analyses in connection with its rulemaking activities,"[71] and said that "the Commission's current rulemaking procedures are closely aligned with the requirements" of the executive order and the circular.[72] The OIG also noted that the SEC's website states that "we take into account benefits and costs in our rulemakings [and] assess alternative regulatory approaches," and that the SEC chairman stated during a congressional hearing in March 2011 that the SEC does conduct cost-benefit analyses.[73]

However, the OIG also pointed out that another SEC commissioner stated in a May 2011 speech that the "Commission has not engaged in a cost-benefit analysis of the rulemakings that were essentially dictated by the law."[74] She reportedly went on to say that "By limiting our cost-benefit analysis to those measures over which the Commission has full discretion, we fail to consider all the costs and benefits that will result from a particular regulatory action."[75]

Federal Deposit Insurance Corporation

The FDIC OIG report noted the applicability of the RFA and the PRA, and said that the "Small Business Regulatory Enforcement Fairness Act also requires the FDIC to conduct cost-benefit analyses of final rules."[76] However, that act only requires agencies to submit a cost-benefit analysis to the Government Accountability Office if the agency has prepared one for the final rule at issue.[77] The report noted that FDIC is not covered by Executive Orders 12866 and 13563 or OMB Circular A-4, but said the agency had issued a *Statement of Policy on the Development and Review of FDIC Regulations and Policies* that "generally addresses the spirit of, and principles found in, the two executive orders and OMB guidance."[78]

In terms of agency-specific requirements, the FDIC OIG report identified Section 302 of the Riegle Community Development and Regulatory Improvement Act (12 U.S.C. §4802(a)), which states:

> In determining the effective date and administrative compliance requirements for new regulations that impose additional reporting, disclosure, or other requirements on insured depository institutions, each Federal banking agency shall consider, consistent with the principles of safety and soundness and the public interest - (1) any administrative burdens that such regulations would place on depository institutions, including small depository institutions and customers of depository institutions; and (2) the benefits of such regulations.

Commodity Futures Trading Commission

The June 2011 CFTC OIG report noted that Section 15(a) of the Commodity Exchange Act (7 U.S.C. §19(a)) requires the agency to consider costs and benefits before issuing certain regulations.[79] Specifically, Section 15(a) states the following:

> Before promulgating a regulation under this chapter ... , the Commission shall consider the costs and benefits of the action of the Commission. The costs and benefits of the proposed Commission action shall be evaluated in light of - (A) considerations of protection of market participants and the public; (B) considerations of the efficiency, competitiveness, and financial integrity of futures markets; (C) considerations of price discovery; (D) considerations of sound risk management practices; and (E) other public interest considerations.[80]

In light of this requirement, in September 2010, the CFTC Office of General Counsel and Office of Chief Economist created a template for a uniform cost-benefit analysis methodology to be used in Dodd-Frank Act proposed rules.[81] That template stated, in part, that Section 15(a) "does not require the Commission to quantify the costs and benefits of a rule or to determine whether the benefits of the order outweigh its costs; rather, it requires that the Commission 'consider' the costs and benefits of its actions."[82] It went on to say that CFTC "could in its discretion determine that, notwithstanding its costs, a particular rule is necessary or appropriate to protect the public interest or to effectuate any of the provisions or accomplish any of the purposes of the Act."

In May 2011, the same two offices developed "Staff Guidance on Cost-Benefit Considerations for Final Rulemakings under the Dodd-Frank Act."[83] In that guidance, CFTC staff were told to "consider costs and benefits in the Final Rulemakings utilizing the principles set forth in Executive Order 13563 in a manner that is reasonably feasible and appropriate, and consistent with the underlying statutory mandate [in Section 15(a) of the Commodity Exchange Act]." Rulemaking teams were allowed to "choose ... quantitative analysis to respond to comments received."[84] The guidance goes on to say that additional analysis is primarily needed when the comments raise specific concerns about costs and benefits, and that "[q]uantitative benefits need not always be greater than costs because there may be a statutory mandate or policy rationale behind the rule."[85]

Comptroller of the Currency

Section 315 of the Dodd-Frank Act amended the PRA (44 U.S.C. §3502(5)) to designate OCC, which is an agency within the Department of the Treasury, as an independent regulatory agency. Prior to the Dodd Frank Act, OCC was not considered an independent regulatory agency and therefore was subject to Executive Order 12866 and OMB Circular A-4, as well as the Unfunded Mandates Reform Act. OCC still remains a component of the Department of the Treasury, but because it is designated as an independent regulatory agency under the PRA, OCC is no longer subject to those requirements.

After discussing the applicability of analytical requirements in the RFA and the PRA, the Treasury OIG report[86] noted requirements in the Riegle Community Development and Regulatory Improvement Act ("Riegle Act," 12 U.S.C. §4802(a)), which states:

> In determining the effective date and administrative compliance requirements for new regulations that impose additional reporting, disclosure, or other requirements on insured depository institutions, each Federal banking agency shall consider, consistent with the principles of safety and soundness and the public interest - (1) any administrative burdens that such regulations would place on depository institutions, including small depository institutions and customers of depository institutions; and (2) the benefits of such regulations.

The term "Federal banking agencies" is defined in Section 4801 of the Riegle Act (12 U.S.C. §1813) as the "Office of the Comptroller of the Currency, the Office of Thrift Supervision, the Board of Governors of the Federal Reserve System, and the Federal Deposit Insurance Corporation." Therefore, although its OIG did not mention it, the Board of Governors of the Federal Reserve System also appears to be covered by this requirement.

Summary of the OIG Reports

Although the OIG reports identified statutory cost-benefit requirements that are applicable to all five of the independent regulatory agencies, those requirements are not as directive or as detailed as those in Executive Order 12866 or OMB Circular A-4. The statutory requirements often only require the agencies to "consider" costs and benefits, but do not specifically require the agencies to conduct a detailed analysis or to demonstrate that the benefits of their rules exceed or justify the costs. For example:

- The National Securities Market Improvement Act requires the SEC to "consider" whether an action "will promote efficiency, competition, and capital formation," and the Securities Exchange Act of 1934 requires the agency to "consider" the impact that a rule would have on competition.
- The Riegle Act requires the FDIC, the OCC, and the Board of Governors of the Federal Reserve System to "consider ... any administrative burdens that such regulations would place on depository institutions ... [and] the benefits of such regulations."
- The Commodities Exchange Act requires CFTC to "consider the costs and benefits of the action of the Commission."

That lack of specificity notwithstanding, however, it is unclear how these agencies will be able to "consider" regulatory costs and benefits if they do not perform some type of systematic economic analysis of their proposed regulations. In the previously mentioned July 2011 decision by the U.S. Court of Appeals for the District of Columbia involving an SEC rule, the court said that the agency has a "statutory obligation to determine as best it can the economic implications of the rule."[87]

Consumer Financial Protection Bureau

Although not included in the 10 Senators' May 4 letter to the OIGs, the Bureau of Consumer Financial Protection (often referred to as the Consumer Financial Protection Bureau, or CFPB) within the Federal Reserve System is also expected to issue Dodd-Frank Act regulations that will be of interest to financial institutions, the public, and Congress. CFPB was created by Title X of the Dodd-Frank Act, which consolidated many federal consumer protection responsibilities into the bureau. The act transferred supervisory and enforcement authority over a number of consumer financial products and services to the bureau on July 21, 2011. Title X and Title XIV of the act contain numerous provisions that require or permit the CFPB to issue regulations implementing the statute's provisions.[88]

Section 1022(b)(2)(A) of the Dodd-Frank Act (12 U.S.C. §5512) establishes certain "standards of rulemaking" for CFPB. Specifically, it states that

> the Bureau shall consider—(i) the potential benefits and costs to consumers and covered persons, including the potential reduction of access by consumers to consumer financial products or services resulting

from such rule; and (ii) the impact of proposed rules on covered persons, as described in section 1026, and the impact on consumers in rural areas.

Therefore, CFPB, like the other banking agencies, appears to be required to "consider" costs and benefits before issuing its rules, but is not specifically required to prepare detailed cost-benefit analyses to accomplish that goal.

Consumer Product Safety Commission

On July 7, 2011, the Subcommittee on Oversight and Investigations of the House Committee on Energy and Commerce held a hearing at which several independent regulatory agencies testified about their response to the issuance of Executive Order 13563.[89] One of the agencies represented at the hearing was the Consumer Product Safety Commission (CPSC). CPSC Commissioner Robert S. Adler testified that the commission has been required since 1981 amendments to the Consumer Product Safety Act to "conduct an extensive cost-benefit analysis when we promulgate safety rules." He said these provisions "easily match, if not surpass, in their stringency and scope the cost-benefit provisions of the various executive orders on cost-benefit analysis recommended by the Office of Management and Budget." Specifically, he noted a number of provisions in the agency's organic statute that require the CPSC to conduct a regulatory analysis prior to issuing a consumer product safety rule.[90] Commissioner Adler also noted, however, that the agency has issued only nine mandatory safety rules in the last 30 years, "opting instead to work with the voluntary standards sector and to negotiate individual Corrective Action Plans for the recall of specific hazardous products."[91] He also said that certain labeling requirements do not require the same level of regulatory analysis as other types of safety rules.

Another perspective was offered by CPSC Commissioner Anne M. Northup, who said that most of the regulations mandated by the Consumer Product Safety Improvement Act of 2008 (CPSIA) are not required to be issued pursuant to the above-mentioned provisions that require cost-benefit analysis, and that the commission "has never conducted a full cost-benefit analysis of any regulation we have promulgated under the CPSIA."[92] She also said that such an analysis would reveal that many of the regulations that the act required to be issued "cannot be justified."

IMPLEMENTATION OF COST-BENEFIT REQUIREMENTS

As noted previously in this report, Executive Order 12866 requires covered agencies to prepare cost-benefit analyses only if their rules are expected to be "economically significant" or "major" (e.g., are expected to have a $100 million annual effect on the economy). A 2011 CRS report examined 100 rules issued during calendar year 2010 that OIRA and the agencies considered to be "major," and concluded that 37 of the rules appeared to be major because they involved annual transfers of $100 million in funds from one party to another party, most commonly the transfer of federal funds to the recipients of those funds (e.g., grants, food stamps, Medicare or Medicaid funds, special pay for members of the military, and crop payments).[93] Ten other rules appeared to be major because they were expected to prompt $100 million or more in annual consumer spending, or because they were establishing fees for the reimbursement of particular federal functions (e.g., issuance of passports and oversight of the nuclear power industry). Thirty-nine rules appeared to be major because they were expected to result in at least $100 million in annual compliance costs, regulatory benefits, or both. In 20 of those 39 rules, estimated annual costs and benefits were both expected to exceed $100 million. In 14 of the 20 rules, the agencies' lowest estimates of regulatory benefits were larger than the highest estimated compliance costs. In only one rule were the lowest costs greater than the highest benefits, and the agency indicated that this result was caused by the lack of discretion provided in the underlying statute.[94]

OMB Annual Reports on Costs and Benefits

OMB's annual reports on the costs and benefits of regulations also indicate the extent to which federal agencies are estimating the costs and benefits of their rules.[95] In the 2013 report, reflecting rules issued during FY2012, OMB reported that executive agencies issued a total of 47 major final rules.[96] Twenty-two of these rules are considered "transfer" rules, which involve monetary transfers. The issuing agencies quantified the amount of the transfer for all but two of these rules. For 14 of the remaining 25 rules, the issuing agencies quantified and monetized both benefits and costs, with annual costs estimated to be between $14.8 billion and $19.5 billion, and annual benefits estimated at between $53.2 billion and $114.6 billion. For the other 11 rules, the agencies monetized only costs or benefits, but not both.

The OMB report also indicated that independent regulatory agencies issued 23 major final rules during FY2012. Seventeen of these 23 rules included some information on the associated costs and benefits. Seven of these rules provided monetized costs, while none provided monetized benefits. The SEC monetized costs for 3 of its 5 rules and 2 of the 3 rules that were issued jointly with the CFTC. The CFTC issued 10 rules in FY2012, 2 of which had monetized costs. There were also 2 rules issued by the CFPB, which included neither monetized costs nor benefits. OMB said that even when these agencies did cost-benefit analyses, it did "not know whether the rigor of the analyses conducted by these agencies is similar to that of the analyses performed by agencies subject to OMB review."[97] OMB went on say the following:

> We emphasize that for the purposes of informing the public and obtaining full accounting, it would be desirable to obtain better information on the benefits and costs of the rules issued by independent regulatory agencies. The absence of such information is a continued obstacle to transparency, and it might also have adverse effects on public policy.[98]

Previous OMB Reports

Previous OMB reports evidenced the same patterns of analysis. For example:

- In the 2012 report (reflecting rules issued during FY20011), OMB reported that executive agencies issued 53 major final rules, of which 30 were budgetary transfers. For 12 of the remaining 23 rules, both costs and benefits were quantified, with estimated benefits between \$34.3 billion and \$89.5 billion and estimated costs between \$5.0 billion and \$10.1 billion. For nine additional rules, the issuing agency was able to identify either costs or benefits, but not both. Independent regulatory agencies issued 17 major final rules in FY2011. None of these included monetized benefits, while six included monetized costs (one from the NRC and five from the SEC).[99]
- In the 2011 report (reflecting rules issued during FY2010), OMB reported that executive agencies issued 66 major final rules. Thirty-two of these rules were budgetary transfers. Eighteen of these rules included monetized costs and benefits, with combined estimated benefits between \$18.8 billion and \$86.1 billion and estimated costs between \$6.5 billion and \$12.5 billion. For 10 additional rules, the

issuing agency monetized costs or benefits, but not both. Independent regulatory agencies issued 17 major final rules. None of these rules included monetized benefits, while eight included monetized costs. Six of these rules were issued by the SEC, one was issued by the NRC, and one was jointly issued by the Federal Reserve System and the FTC.[100]

Appendix C of the 2013 OMB report provided information on the number of major rules issued by independent regulatory agencies during the 10-year period from October 1, 2003, through September 30, 2012. That information, shown in **Table 2** below, indicates that 64% of agency rules included information on either associated costs or benefits.

Table 2. Independent Regulatory Agencies and Cost-Benefit Analysis: FY2003 Through FY2012

Agency	Major Rules Issued	Major Rules with Some Benefit or Cost Information
Consumer Financial Protection Bureau	2	2
Commodity Futures Trading Commission	11	8
Commodity Futures Trading Commission/Securities and Exchange Commission	3	2
Consumer Product Safety Commission	3	1
Federal Communications Commission	13	1
Federal Deposit Insurance Commission/Federal Reserve System/Office of the Comptroller of the Currency	1	0
Federal Energy Regulatory Commission	1	1
Federal Reserve System	16	3
Federal Trade Commission	2	1
Nuclear Regulatory Commission	12	4
Securities and Exchange Commission	54	53
Total	118	76

Source: OMB's 2013 report on costs and benefits, Appendix C.

The CRS and OMB reports suggest several broad conclusions about the current state of regulatory analysis. First, many of the rules for which agencies are required to prepare cost-benefit analyses are "major" for reasons unrelated to regulatory compliance costs. Therefore, although economic analyses of these rules may be appropriate for transparency or other reasons, it may be unlikely that the analyses will result in significantly reduced compliance costs or increased regulatory benefits. Second, Cabinet departments and independent agencies like EPA are more likely to prepare cost-benefit analyses that produce monetized estimates of costs and benefits than independent regulatory agencies. However, not all rules issued by Cabinet departments and independent agencies contained such estimates. When monetary estimates of costs and benefits are available, estimated benefits are generally higher than estimated costs. Finally, some independent regulatory agencies (e.g., the SEC and the NRC) appear to be more likely to estimate at least the costs of their regulations than other independent regulatory agencies (e.g., the FCC and the Federal Reserve System).

December 2013 GAO Report

In December 2013, GAO published a report on regulatory analyses conducted for rules issued under the Dodd-Frank Wall Street Reform and Consumer Protection Act.[101] In that report, GAO concluded that the agencies issuing rules under Dodd-Frank generally completed the analyses that were required in those rules. Most of the agencies issuing rules under Dodd-Frank are independent regulatory agencies, and, as such, were sometimes required to conduct analyses under the PRA and the RFA. GAO examined a total of 59 "substantive" rules, 10 of which were "major." For the major rules, according to GAO, agencies generally relied on the key elements of OMB Circular A-4 in conducting their analyses.

REGULATORY REFORM LEGISLATION IN THE 113TH CONGRESS

A number of bills were introduced in the 113th Congress that would codify, expand, or otherwise modify existing requirements for cost-benefit or other types of regulatory impact analysis. Some of the bills would expand the principles and requirements in Executive Order 12866 to all agencies or rules, some would require cost-benefit analysis by certain agencies, and other bills would modify the analytical requirements in the RFA or UMRA. A few examples of these bills are listed below.[102]

- H.R. 899, the Unfunded Mandates Information and Transparency Act of 2014, would amend the current analysis requirements in UMRA by making those requirements more broad (i.e., by requiring them to be completed for a greater number of rules) and by requiring a more detailed level of analysis.
- H.R. 2122, the Regulatory Accountability Act of 2013, would make several changes to the rulemaking process by amending the Administrative Procedure Act (APA). Among those changes would be a requirement for agencies to conduct cost-benefit analysis when issuing rules, which is not currently required under the APA.
- H.R. 2542, the Regulatory Flexibility Improvements Act of 2013, would amend and expand current analysis requirements under the RFA.
- H.R. 3863 and S. 2099, the Sound Regulation Act of 2014, would amend the APA to require that agencies conduct cost-benefit analysis when issuing rules.
- H.R. 5184 and S. 2153, the National Regulatory Budget Act of 2014, would establish an Office of Regulatory Analysis as an independent establishment in the executive branch that would be required to conduct its own cost-benefit analysis.
- S. 1173, the Independent Agency Regulatory Analysis Act of 2014, would authorize the President to subject independent regulatory agencies to cost-benefit analysis requirements that exist in executive order (discussed above) and do not currently apply to independent regulatory agencies.

CONCLUDING OBSERVATIONS

As the preceding discussion indicates, many federal agencies are already required to conduct cost-benefit and other types of analysis before they issue certain proposed or final rules. These requirements have been added incrementally by various statutes and executive orders during the past 40 to 50 years, and sometimes require agencies to perform the same general types of analyses. For example, virtually all of the elements of the written statements that agencies are required to prepare pursuant to UMRA were already required by Executive Order 12866 (e.g., quantitative and qualitative estimates of costs and benefits, effects on the national economy, consideration of a range of alternatives, selection of the alternative that is least costly, most cost-effective, or least burdensome, or an explanation of why that alternative was not selected). The drafters of UMRA appear to have recognized the overlap, stating in Section 202(c) of the statute (2 U.S.C. §1534) that an agency may prepare the written statement "in conjunction with or as part of any other statement or analysis." Section 605(a) of the RFA (5 U.S.C. §605(a)) contains the same type of statement.

Also, many of the current requirements have substantial exclusions and exceptions, or give federal agencies substantial discretion to decide whether an analysis is required. For example, the RFA's analytical requirements do not apply to rules that are issued without a prior notice of proposed rulemaking, and agencies can avoid regulatory flexibility analyses if they certify that their rules do not have a "significant" economic impact on a "substantial" number of small entities. UMRA does not apply to independent regulatory agencies, and contains more than a dozen other ways that "economically significant" rules would not be covered by its requirements. Executive orders on children, federalism, and energy permit agencies to escape coverage of their analytical requirements if they conclude the effects of their rules will not have "disproportionate" effects on children, will not have "significant federalism implications," or do not involve "significant energy actions." Executive Order 12866 and OMB Circular A-4 contain some of the most inclusive and far-reaching analytical requirements, but they do not apply to independent regulatory agencies, or to rules that are not "economically significant."

Congressional Options

Congress could decide to keep the existing analytical framework in place. Alternatively, Congress could decide to enact one or more of the bills listed above, perhaps resulting in more analyses being performed, more detailed analyses, or both. Some of these bills would result in substantial changes to the current requirements discussed above, while other bills would not substantially change the nature or number of regulatory analyses that certain agencies would perform. Finally, enacting one or more of the bills would add to the existing, incrementally developed combination of statutes, executive orders, and OMB circulars that covers some agencies and rules but not others, and could potentially be confusing to agencies and the public.

Another, more comprehensive approach could be to consolidate all of the analytical requirements in one place, and perhaps expand those requirements to include more agencies or more rules, or to require different types of analysis for the rules that are covered. Since Executive Order 12866 and OMB Circular A-4 currently contain the most detailed and inclusive analytical requirements, perhaps the easiest way to accomplish that goal would be to add elements to the executive order and circular and ensure that certain agencies and types of economic effects are included (e.g., effects on small entities, or state, local, or tribal governments). The President could arguably make most of these changes by amending the executive order and the circular without congressional action.[103] In 2011, OMB said obtaining better information on the costs and benefits of independent regulatory agencies' rules was "desirable," and described the absence of such information as an "obstacle to transparency" that may be having "adverse effects on public policy."[104] For more than 20 years, the Administrative Conference of the United States and the American Bar Association have recommended that independent regulatory agencies' rules be reviewed by OIRA.[105]

However, expanding the executive order's cost-benefit analysis requirements to independent regulatory agencies, and requiring those agencies to submit their covered rules and analyses to OIRA for review, may trigger resistance by those in Congress and elsewhere who believe these agencies should remain more independent of presidential influence than Cabinet departments or agencies like EPA. Sally Katzen, OIRA Administrator for five years during the Clinton Administration, favors expansion of the executive order's requirements to independent regulatory agencies, and has suggested that a "sense of the Congress" resolution indicating that such a course would be desirable "would go a long way to ameliorate any concerns in that regard."[106]

Another option would be to amend the executive order to require independent regulatory agencies to prepare cost-benefit analyses, but not require them to submit their rules to OIRA for review.[107] If Congress was to establish a "congressional office of regulatory analysis" as is contemplated in H.R. 214 from the 112th Congress (introduced by Representative Don Young on January 7, 2011), then perhaps the rules and analyses could be submitted there.[108] Or, to maintain a measure of independence, the independent regulatory agencies could be required to submit their rules and analyses to

OIRA, but the agencies could be given the same type of authority they have with regard to PRA submissions—to override any objections from OIRA by a majority vote of the agency's leadership.[109]

Codification of Executive Order's Requirements

Alternatively, Congress could decide to enact legislation codifying and expanding the executive order's requirements to cover independent regulatory agencies, and requiring different types of analyses. Supporters of this approach include Susan Dudley, OIRA Administrator for two years during the George W. Bush Administration, who has said codification could (1) signal congressional support for cost-benefit analysis principles, (2) apply the requirements to independent regulatory agencies, and (3) make compliance with the requirements judicially reviewable.[110] She also said that legislation could emphasize certain types of analyses that have been found lacking (e.g., effects on employment or indirect effects). Support has also come from Professor Peter L. Strauss of Columbia Law School, who testified in February 2011 that codifying in one statute the analytic requirements in Executive Order 12866 and elsewhere, and "framing them to permit needed regulation to proceed efficiently, would in my judgment be a highly desirable step.[111]

Other observers, however, have opposed codification of the cost-benefit analysis requirements in Executive Order 12866. For example, Sally Katzen has said that (1) the executive order's requirements have been successfully implemented for more than 30 years (as evidenced by the fact that OMB's reports regularly show that the costs of rules exceed the benefits); (2) even if the executive orders were not working well, there is no evidence that putting the requirements in statutes would make them work better; (3) the executive orders permit Presidents to emphasize different things during their administrations, which would be lost if the requirements were put in statute; and (4) codification of cost-benefit analysis requirements "would be amending a host of previously enacted statutes that either are silent on the role of costs in the formulation of regulations or do not permit the consideration of such factors."[112]

Another option to cover all or some of the independent regulatory agencies by the requirements of Executive Order 12866 would be for Congress to amend the statutory definition of an "independent regulatory agency" that is referenced in the executive order. Executive Order 12866 defines an "agency" as (unless otherwise indicated) "any authority of the United States that is an 'agency' under 44 U.S.C. §3502(1), other than those considered to be independent regulatory agencies, as defined in 44 U.S.C. §3502(10)." That definition (which is actually in 44 U.S.C. §3502(5)) lists the agencies considered to be independent regulatory agencies (e.g., CFTC, SEC, FCC, and the NRC), and also says it includes "any other similar agency designated by statute as a Federal independent regulatory agency or commission." Congress could amend this provision, stating that, for purposes of Executive Order 12866, all or certain of these agencies would be covered by the analytical and/or rule submission requirements in the executive order.[113] This approach would not, however, prohibit the President or any future President from amending or revoking the executive order.

Contextual Considerations

Whether done by presidential or congressional action, any effort to consolidate or reform the analytical requirements in rulemaking should be cognizant of the state of existing law in this area. Congress has required cost-benefit analysis in some statutes, prohibited it in other statutes,[114] and not precluded it in still other statutes.[115] Both Executive Orders 12866 and 13563 contain the phrase "to the extent permitted by law" when referencing the principles of rulemaking and the analytical requirements, confirming that agencies must adhere to the requirements contained in their authorizing statutes, and may only apply the principles and procedures of the executive orders if the statutes permit them to do so. Should Congress decide to enact legislation superseding existing law, it should do so in full recognition of the likely consequences.

Presidential and congressional requirements for cost-benefit analysis should also recognize that data availability may be an implementation issue, and that additional resources may be necessary for the agencies conducting these analyses. In some cases, the data that agencies need to estimate the costs and benefits of their rules may not exist, or may only be available from regulated entities.[116] Although there is no "typical" cost-benefit analysis (just as there is no "typical" rule), the cost of conducting many individual regulatory analyses has been in the hundreds of thousands of dollars.[117] If more agencies were required to prepare more detailed analyses for more rules, it is likely that the agencies would make the argument that they would be unable to do so without additional resources.[118]

End Notes

[1] See, for example, Tammy O. Tengs and John D. Graham, "The Opportunity Costs of Haphazard Social Investments in Life-Saving," in *Risks, Costs, and Lives Saved: Getting Better Results from Regulation*, Robert W. Hahn, ed. (New York: Oxford University Press, 1996). For a counter argument, see Richard W. Parker, "Grading the Government," *The University of Chicago Law Review*, vol. 70 (Fall 2003), pp. 1345-1486.

[2] See, for example, Cass R. Sunstein, *The Cost-Benefit State: The Future of Regulatory Protection* (Chicago: American Bar Association, 2002); and Robert W. Hahn and Cass R. Sunstein, "A New Executive Order for Improving Federal Regulation? Deeper and Wider Cost-Benefit Analysis," Working Paper 02-4, AEI-Brookings Joint Center for Regulatory Studies, March 2002.

[3] See, for example, Lisa Heinzerling and Frank Ackerman, *Pricing the Priceless: Cost-Benefit Analysis of Environmental Protection* (Washington: Georgetown University, 2002).

[4] *Whitman v. American Trucking Associations*, 531 U.S. 457 (2001).

[5] *Entergy Corp. v. Riverkeeper, Inc.*, 556 U.S. 208 (2009).

[6] See Kenneth J. Arrow, et al., *Benefit-Cost Analysis in Environmental, Health, and Safety Regulation: A Statement of Principles* (Annapolis: The Annapolis Center, 1996). More recently, an analysis of the comments submitted to the Office of Management and Budget in 2009 regarding possible changes to Executive Order 12866 concluded that none of the commenting regulatory scholars advocated that cost-benefit analysis should be abandoned, or that cost-benefit analysis alone should be the determinative factor in regulatory decisionmaking. See Helen G. Boutrous, "Regulatory Review in the Obama Administration: Cost-Benefit Analysis for Everyone," *Administrative Law Review*, vol. 62 (Winter 2010), pp. 252-253.

[7] Various studies have been done over the years assessing the quality of agencies' cost-benefit analyses. See, for example, U.S. General Accounting Office, *Regulatory Reform: Agencies Could Improve Development, Documentation, and Clarity of Regulatory Economic Analyses,* GAO/RCED-98-142, May 26, 1998; Richard D. Morgenstern, ed., *Economic Analyses at EPA: Assessing Regulatory Impact* (Washington: Resources for the Future, 1997); and Robert W. Hahn, ed., *Risks, Costs, and Lives Saved: Getting Better Results from Regulation* (Washington: AEI Press, 1996).

[8] As used in this report, the term "independent regulatory agencies" refers to the boards and commissions identified as such in the Paperwork Reduction Act (44 U.S.C. § 3502(5)), including the SEC, the FCC, the NRC, and the Federal Energy Regulatory Commission. The term "independent agencies" refers to other agencies that answer directly to the President, but are not part of Cabinet departments (e.g., EPA, the Social Security Administration, and the General Services Administration).

[9] For more information on this initiative, see http://www.thecre.com/ombpapers/20060130_nixon.html.

[10] Executive Order 11821, "Inflation Impact Statements," 39 *Federal Register* 41501, November 29, 1974.

[11] Executive Order 12044, "Improving Government Regulations," 43 *Federal Register* 12661, March 24, 1978.

[12] Executive Order 12291, "Federal Regulation," 46 *Federal Register* 13193, February 19, 1981.

[13] Executive Order 12866, "Regulatory Planning and Review," 58 *Federal Register* 51735, October 4, 1993. To view a copy of this order, see http://www.whitehouse.gov/omb/inforeg/eo12866.pdf.

[14] Section 3(b) of Executive Order 12866 states that "'Agency,' unless otherwise indicated, means any authority of the United States that is an "agency" under 44 U.S.C. 3502(1), other than those considered to be independent regulatory agencies, as defined in 44 U.S.C. 3502(10)." Although the cost-benefit and rule submission requirements in the executive order do not apply to independent regulatory agencies, some parts do (e.g., Section 4(b) relating to the Unified Regulatory Agenda, and Section 4(c) relating to the Regulatory Plan).

[15] The requirement that agencies adopt regulations only if the benefits "justify" the costs was seen as a somewhat different threshold than the one in Executive Order 12291, which had required agencies to determine that regulatory benefits "outweigh" the costs.

[16] Section 3(f) of Executive Order 12866.

[17] The definition of an "economically significant" regulatory action is very similar to the definition of a "major rule" under the Congressional Review Act (5 U.S.C. § 804(2)): "(A) an annual effect on the economy of $100,000,000 or more; (B) a major increase in costs or prices for consumers, individual industries, Federal, State, or local government agencies, or geographic regions; or (C) significant adverse effects on competition, employment, investment, productivity, innovation, or on the ability of United States-based enterprises to compete with foreign-based enterprises in domestic and export markets."

[18] Section 3(a)(3)(D) of Executive Order 12866.

[19] The Administrative Procedure Act (APA) provides that "final agency action for which there is no other adequate remedy in a court [is] subject to judicial review." 5 U.S.C. §§ 702, 704. Judicial review may be invoked under the APA if a plaintiff is "adversely affected or aggrieved" by any final agency action "within the meaning" of the statute at issue. 5 U.S.C. § 702. For more information, see CRS Report R41546, *A Brief Overview of Rulemaking and Judicial Review*, by Todd Garvey and Daniel T. Shedd.

[20] This "best practices" document was developed by an interagency group co-chaired by the Administrator of OIRA and a member of the Council of Economic Advisors. The document was revised and issued as guidance in 2000. To view a copy of the best practices document, see http://www.whitehouse.gov/omb/inforeg/riaguide.html.

[21] OMB Circular A-4, "Regulatory Analysis," September 17, 2003. The circular is available at http://www.whitehouse.gov/omb/assets/regulatory_matters_pdf/a-4.pdf. The circular took effect for economically significant proposed rules on January 1, 2004, and for economically significant final rules on January 1, 2005.

[22] Ibid., p. 1.

[23] Ibid., p. 2.

[24] For example, if Option A has expected costs of $100 million and expected benefits of $200 million, the net benefits are $100 million. If Option B has expected costs of $200 million, and expected benefits of $400 million, the net benefits are $200 million. In this scenario, Option B produces the largest net benefits.

[25] OMB Circular A-4, p. 10.

[26] Lisa Heinzerling and Frank Ackerman, "Pricing the Priceless: Cost-Benefit Analysis of Environmental Protection," Georgetown University, 2002.

[27] For a summary of those efforts, see CRS Report R41140, *How Agencies Monetize "Statistical Lives" Expected to Be Saved By Regulations*, by Curtis W. Copeland.

[28] Ibid.

[29] OMB Circular A-4, p. 11.

[30] Ibid., p. 40.

[31] In 2001, Section 624 of the Treasury and General Government Appropriations Act, 2001, (31 U.S.C. § 1105 note), sometimes known as the "Regulatory Right-to-Know Act," put in place a permanent requirement for an OMB report on regulatory costs and benefits. Specifically, it requires OMB to prepare and submit with the President's budget an "accounting statement and associated report" containing an estimate of the total costs and benefits (including quantifiable and nonquantifiable effects) of federal rules and paperwork, to the extent feasible, (1) in the aggregate, (2) by agency and agency program, and (3) by major rule. The accounting statement is also required to contain an analysis of the impacts of federal regulation on state, local, and tribal governments, small businesses, wages, and economic growth.

[32] Executive Order 13563, "Improving Regulations and Regulatory Review," 76 *Federal Register* 3821, January 21, 2011.

[33] Memorandum from Cass R. Sunstein, Administrator of OIRA, "Executive Order 13563, 'Improving Regulation and Regulatory Review'," February 2, 2011, available at http://www.whitehouse.gov/sites/default/files/omb/memoranda/2011/m11-10.pdf.

[34] Executive Order 13579, "Regulation and Independent Regulatory Agencies," 76 *Federal Register* 41587, July 14, 2011.

[35] See http://www.whitehouse.gov/the-press-office/2011/07/11/memorandum-regulation-and-independent-regulatoryagencies.

[36] Executive Order 13045, "Protection of Children From Environmental Health Risks and Safety Risks," 62 *Federal Register* 19883, April 23, 1997.

[37] Executive Order 13132, "Federalism," 64 *Federal Register* 43255, August 10, 1999.

[38] Executive Order 12612, the previous executive order on federalism, also gave federal agencies broad discretion to determine the applicability of its requirements. GAO examined the implementation of this order and concluded that its analytical requirements were rarely implemented. See U.S. General Accounting Office, *Federalism: Previous Initiatives Have Had Little Effect on Agency Rulemaking*, GAO/T-GGD-99-3, June 30, 1999.

[39] Executive Order 13175, "Consultation and Coordination with Indian Tribal Governments," 65 *Federal Register* 67249, November 9, 2000. This executive order was re-emphasized in a memorandum from President Obama in 2009; see Memorandum for the Heads of Executive Departments and Agencies, "Tribal Consultation," November 5, 2009, at http://www.white house.gov/the-press-office/memorandum-tribal-consultation-signed-president.

[40] Executive Order 13211, "Actions Concerning Regulations That Significantly Affect Energy Supply, Distribution, or Use," 66 *Federal Register* 28355, May 22, 2001.

[41] See http://www.whitehouse.gov/sites/default/files/omb/inforeg/regpol/RIA_Checklist.pdf for a copy of the checklist.

[42] See http://www.whitehouse.gov/sites/default/files/omb/assets/OMB/circulars/a004/a-4_FAQ.pdf for a copy of this document.

[43] See http://www.whitehouse.gov/sites/default/files/omb/inforeg/regpol/circular-a-4_regulatory-impact-analysis-aprimer.pdf for a copy of this document.

[44] 42 U.S.C. § 1302. The department is not required to prepare the analysis if the final rule is issued without a prior notice of proposed rulemaking.

[45] For an overview of UMRA, see CRS Report R40957, *Unfunded Mandates Reform Act: History, Impact, and Issues*, by Robert Jay Dilger and Richard S. Beth.

[46] In recent years, OIRA's annual report on UMRA has been combined with its report on the costs and benefits of federal regulations. See, for example, Office of Management and Budget, Office of Information and Regulatory Affairs, *2010 Report to Congress on the Benefits and Costs of Federal Regulations and Unfunded Mandates on State, Local, and*

Tribal Entities, available at http://www.whitehouse.gov/sites/default/files/omb/legislative/reports/2010_Benefit_Cost_Report.pdf.

[47] U.S. General Accounting Office, *Federal Rulemaking: Agencies Often Published Final Actions Without Proposed Rules*, GAO/GGD-98-126, Aug. 31, 1998.

[48] U.S. General Accounting Office, *Unfunded Mandates: Reform Act Has Had Little Effect on Agencies' Rulemaking Actions*, GAO/GGD-98-30, February 4, 1998.

[49] U.S. General Accounting Office, *Unfunded Mandates: Analysis of Reform Act Coverage*, GAO-04-637, May 12, 2004.

[50] Testimony of Denise M. Fantone, Director, Strategic Issues, U.S. Government Accountability Office, before the Subcommittee on Technology, Information Policy, Intergovernmental Relations and Procurement Reform, House Committee on Oversight of Government Management, available at http://www.gao.gov/products/GAO-11-385T.

[51] For more information, see CRS Report RL33152, *The National Environmental Policy Act (NEPA): Background and Implementation*, by Linda Luther.

[52] CRS Report RS20621, *Overview of National Environmental Policy Act (NEPA) Requirements*, by Kristina Alexander.

[53] Section 1100G of the Dodd-Frank Act added a requirement to § 603 of the RFA that for covered rules, the Consumer Financial Protection Bureau should include of a number of specific items in their impact analysis, including "any projected increase in the cost of credit for small entities."

[54] See, for example, U.S. Department of Health and Human Services, "Patient Protection and Affordable Care Act; Establishment of Consumer Operated and Oriented Plan (CO-OP) Program," 76 *Federal Register* 43237, July 20, 2011, in which the department said that the Centers for Medicare and Medicaid Services interprets the RFA analysis requirement "as applying only to regulations with negative impacts." However, the department said it routinely prepares a voluntary analysis when there are significant positive impacts.

[55] See, for example, *Mid-Tex Electric Cooperative, Inc. v. FERC*, 773 F.2d 327, 343 (D.C. Cir. 1985).

[56] For example, when EPA published a final rule establishing national ambient air quality standards (NAAQS) for particulate matter in October 2006, the agency certified the rule as not triggering the RFA "because NAAQS themselves impose no regulations on small entities." In its cost-benefit analysis for the rule, EPA estimated the cost of installing controls to meet the health standard at $5.6 billion in 2020. See U.S. Environmental Protection Agency, "National Ambient Air Quality Standards for Particulate Matter; Final Rule," 71 *Federal Register* 61144, 61217. (EPA made the same argument in other rules. See U.S. Environmental Protection Agency, "Primary National Ambient Air Quality Standard for Sulfur Dioxide," 74 *Federal Register* 64810, at 64865, December 8, 2009; and "National Ambient Air Quality Standards for Carbon Monoxide," 76 *Federal Register* 8158, at 8195, February 11, 2011.) In a similar case (*American Trucking Associations, Inc. v. U.S. Environmental Protection Agency*, 175 F.3d 1027 (D.C. Cir. 1999)), affirmed in part and reversed in part, *Whitman v. American Trucking Associations*, 532 U.S. 457 (2001), the U.S. Court of Appeals for the District of Columbia ruled that EPA had complied with the RFA because the states, not EPA, had the direct authority to impose requirements to control ozone and particulate matter consistent with EPA health standards.

[57] U.S. General Accounting Office, *Regulatory Flexibility Act: Inherent Weaknesses May Limit Its Usefulness for Small Governments*, GAO/HRD-91-16, January 11, 1991.

[58] U.S. General Accounting Office, *Regulatory Flexibility Act: Status of Agencies' Compliance*, GAO/GGD-94-105, April 27, 1994.

[59] U.S. General Accounting Office, *Regulatory Flexibility Act: Agencies' Interpretations of Review Requirements Vary*, GAO/GGD-99-55, April 2, 1999.

[60] U.S. General Accounting Office, *Regulatory Flexibility Act: Implementation in EPA Program Offices and Proposed Lead Rule*, GAO/GGD-00-193. September 20, 2000, p. 31.

[61] Section 612 of the RFA requires the SBA Chief Counsel for Advocacy to "monitor" agencies' compliance with the RFA, but does not require SBA to issue binding rules defining key terms.

[62] U.S. General Accounting Office, *Regulatory Flexibility Act: Key Terms Still Need to Be Clarified*, GAO-01-669T, April 24, 2001.

[63] See, for example, page 17 of the SBA Office of Advocacy's guidance on the implementation of the RFA, available at http://www.sba.gov/sites/default/files/rfaguide.pdf, which says "Significance should not be viewed in absolute terms...." For more information on the RFA, see CRS Report RL34355, *The Regulatory Flexibility Act: Implementation Issues and Proposed Reforms*, coordinated by Maeve P. Carey.

[64] For example, Environmental Protection Agency's Toxics Release Inventory (TRI) program is essentially a database created through collections of information imposed on businesses to inform the public about chemical hazards in their communities. TRI reports require businesses in certain industries to report the quantity of any of more than 600 chemicals entering each environmental medium on site, transfers of the chemical in wastes to off-site locations, on-site treatment methods and efficiency, and source reduction and recycling activities.

[65] For an up-to-date inventory of OMB-approved information collections, see http://www.reginfo.gov/public/do/PRAMain.

[66] 44 U.S.C. 3507(f). For more information on the PRA, see CRS Report R40636, *Paperwork Reduction Act (PRA): OMB and Agency Responsibilities and Burden Estimates*, by Curtis W. Copeland and Vanessa K. Burrows. The authors of that report have left CRS; questions about its content may be directed to the coordinator of this report, Maeve P. Carey.

[67] The Senators also asked the OIGs to describe internal policies and procedures governing economic analyses of proposed rules, the degree to which agency staff understand and follow applicable requirements, the qualifications of the staff who conduct the analyses, and other aspects of those analyses.

[68] Office of the Inspector General, Board of Governors of the Federal Reserve System, "Response to a Congressional Request Regarding the Economic Analysis Associated with Specified Rulemakings," June 13, 2011, p. 6.

[69] Ibid., p. 7.

[70] Office of the Inspector General, U.S. Securities and Exchange Commission, "Report of Review of Economic Analyses Performed by the Securities and Exchange Commission in Connection with Dodd-Frank Rulemakings," June 13, 2011, available at http://www.sec-oig.gov/Reports/AuditsInspections/2011/Report_6_13_11.pdf (hereinafter referred to as "OIG/SEC").

[71] In support of this statement, the OIG noted that SEC Office of General Counsel officials quoted former SEC Chairman Arthur Levitt, who said there was an expectation that the SEC would perform cost-benefit analyses as part of the rulemaking process. See OIG/SEC, p. 4.

[72] OIG/SEC, p. 4.

[73] Ibid., p. 5, citing testimony by SEC Chairman Mary Shapiro before the Subcommittee on Financial Services and General Government, House Committee on Appropriations, March 15, 2011.

[74] Ibid., pp. 5-6, citing a speech by Commissioner Kathleen Casey at an SEC open meeting regarding rules for Nationally Recognized Statistical Rating Organizations held on May 18, 2011.

[75] In a somewhat related development, on July 22, 2011, the U.S. Court of Appeals for the District of Columbia vacated an SEC final rule on proxy access, saying the Commission acted arbitrarily and capriciously for having failed to assess the economic implications of a rule adequately. *Business Roundtable v. SEC*, D.C. Cir., No 10-1305, July 22, 2010. In particular, the Court said (on p. 7 of the opinion) that the SEC had "inconsistently and opportunistically framed the costs and benefits of the rule; failed adequately to quantify the certain costs or to explain why those costs could not be quantified; neglected to support its predictive judgments; contradicted itself; and failed to respond to substantial problems raised by commenters." Citing an earlier case (C*hamber of Commerce v. SEC*, 412 F.3d 133, 143 (D.C. Cir. 2005)), the Court said that the agency has a "statutory obligation to determine as best it can the economic implications of the rule." Some observers believe that this case has "elevated the importance of economic analysis in rulemaking to implement" the Dodd-Frank Act. See, for example, Yin Wilczek, "D.C. Circuit's Proxy Access Ruling Raises Importance of Economic Review, Panel Says," *BNA Daily Report for Executives*, August 2, 2011, p. EE-4; and David S. Hilzenrath, "Wall Street Finds Relief in Court from SEC Rules," *Washington Post*, August 12, 2011, p. A-10.

[76] Office of the Inspector General, Federal Deposit Insurance Corporation, "Evaluation of the FDIC's Economic Analysis of Three Rulemakings to Implement Provisions of the Dodd-Frank Act," Report No. EVAL-11-003, June 2011, p. 1 of the Executive Summary. The report is available at http://www.fdicoig.gov/reports11%5C11-003EV.pdf, and is hereinafter referred to as "OIG/FDIC."

[77] Specifically, the portion of SBREFA known as the Congressional Review Act states that rulemaking agencies must submit to GAO, and make available to each house of Congress, "a complete copy of the cost-benefit analysis of the rule, if any" (5 U.S.C. 801(a)(1)(b)(i)).

[78] OIG/FDIC, p. 1 of the Executive Summary.

[79] Office of the Inspector General, U.S. Commodity Futures Trading Commission, "A Review of Cost-Benefit Analyses Performed by the Commodity Futures Trading Commission in Connection with Rulemakings Undertaken Pursuant to the Dodd-Frank Act," June 13, 2011, available at http://www.cftc.gov/ucm/groups/public/@aboutcftc/documents/file/oig_investigation_061311.pdf, and is hereinafter referred to as "OIG/CFTC." The CFTC OIG had previously issued an April 15, 2011, report in response to a congressional request entitled "An Investigation Regarding the Cost-Benefit Analyses Performed by the Commodity Futures Trading Commission in Connection with Rulemakings Undertaken Pursuant to the Dodd-Frank Act," available at http://www.cftc.gov/ucm/groups/public/@aboutcftc/documents/file/oig_investigation_041511.pdf.

[80] Subsection (a)(3) states that these requirements do not apply to "(A) An order that initiates, is part of, or is the result of an adjudicatory or investigative process of the Commission. (B) An emergency action. (C) A finding of fact regarding compliance with a requirement of the Commission."

[81] OIG/CFTC, Exhibit 1.

[82] OIG/CFTC, p. 3.

[83] Ibid., Exhibit 2.

[84] Ibid., Exhibit 2, p. 3.

[85] Ibid., Exhibit 2, pp. 6-7.

[86] Office of the Inspector General, Department of the Treasury, "Dodd-Frank Act: Congressional Request for Information Regarding Economic Analysis by OCC," June 13, 2011, available at http://www.treasury.gov/about/organizational-structure/ig/Documents/OIG-CA-11-006.pdf.

[87] *Business Roundtable v. SEC*, D.C. Cir., No 10-1305, July 22, 2010, citing *Chamber of Commerce v. SEC*, 412 F.3d 133, 143 (D.C. Cir. 2005).

[88] For information on the rules that CFPB are expected to issue, see CRS Report R41380, *The Dodd-Frank Wall Street Reform and Consumer Protection Act: Regulations to be Issued by the Consumer Financial Protection Bureau*, by Curtis W. Copeland. For more information on CFPB itself, see CRS Report R41338, *The Dodd-Frank Wall Street Reform and Consumer Protection Act: Title X, The Consumer Financial Protection Bureau*, by David H. Carpenter.

[89] U.S. Congress, House Committee on Energy and Commerce, Subcommittee on Oversight and Investigations, *The Views of the Independent Agencies on Regulatory Reform*, 112th Cong., 1st sess., July 7, 2011, H.Hrg. 112-71 (Washington: GPO, 2011).

[90] 15 U.S.C. §2058(f).

[91] Ibid., pp. 13-28.

[92] Ibid., pp. 29-53.

[93] CRS Report R41651, *REINS Act: Number and Types of "Major Rules" in Recent Years*, by Maeve P. Carey and Curtis W. Copeland. The definitions of "economically significant" and "major" are almost identical.

[94] Other rules appeared to be considered major because of increased costs or prices (albeit less than $100 million per year), or for multiple reasons.

[95] In 2001, Section 624 of the Treasury and General Government Appropriations Act, 2001, (31 U.S.C. § 1105 note), sometimes known as the "Regulatory Right-to-Know Act," put in place a permanent requirement for an OMB report on regulatory costs and benefits. Specifically, it requires OMB to prepare and submit with the President's budget an "accounting statement and associated report" containing an estimate of the total costs and benefits (including quantifiable and nonquantifiable effects) of federal rules and paperwork, to the extent feasible, (1) in the aggregate, (2) by agency and agency program, and (3) by major rule.

[96] Office of Management and Budget, *2013 Report to Congress on the Benefits and Costs of Federal Regulations and Unfunded Mandates on State, Local, and Tribal Entities*, May 2013, available at http://www.whitehouse.gov/sites/default/files/omb/inforeg/2013_cb/2013_cost_benefit_report-updated.pdf.

[97] Ibid., p. 35.

[98] Ibid.

[99] See http://www.whitehouse.gov/sites/default/files/omb/inforeg/2012_cb/2012_cost_benefit_report.pdf for a copy of this report.

[100] See http://www.whitehouse.gov/sites/default/files/omb/inforeg/2011_cb/2011_cba_ report.pdf for a copy of this report.

[101] U.S. Government Accountability Office, *Agencies Conducted Regulatory Analyses and Coordinated by Could Benefit from Additional Guidance on Major Rules*, GAO-14-67, December 2013, http://www.gao.gov/assets/660/659586.pdf.

[102] Not included in this list are bills whose primary purpose is something other than changing regulatory impact analysis requirements, or bills that would change regulatory analysis requirements for one agency or a small group of agencies (e.g., financial regulators).

103 Commenters at an April 2011 Resources for the Future conference stated that both President Reagan and President Clinton obtained legal opinions from the Office of Legal Counsel at the Department of Justice stating that Executive Orders 12291 and 12866 could cover independent regulatory agencies. However, according to Sally Katzen, President Clinton's OIRA Administrator, the decision not to cover them was reportedly a political, not a legal, determination. See http://www.rff.org/Documents/Events/Workshops%20and%20 Conferences/110407_Regulation_KatzenRemarks.pdf, pp. 2-3.

[104] Office of Management and Budget, *2011 Report to Congress on the Benefits and Costs of Federal Regulations and Unfunded Mandates on State, Local, and Tribal Entities*, June 2011, p. 31, available at http://www.whitehouse.gov/sites/default/files/omb/inforeg/ 2011_cb/2011_cba_report.pdf.

[105] Administrative Conference of the United States, ACUS Recommendation 88-1, "Presidential Review of Agency Rulemaking," 1988, available at http://www.law.fsu.edu/ library/ admin/acus/305889.html. Comments from the American Bar Association on presidential supervision on rulemaking, March 16, 2009 (citing House of Delegates, Recommendation: Presidential Review of Rulemaking (Annual Meeting 1990)), available at http://www. reginfo.gov/public/jsp/EO/fedRegReview/ABANET_comments.pdf. See also the American Bar Association's statement in support of S. 1173, the Independent Agency Regulatory Analysis Act of 2013, at http://www.americanbar.org/content/dam/aba/ uncategorized/ GAO/2013sept16_indregagencies_l.authcheckdam.pdf.

[106] Testimony of Sally Katzen before the Senate Committee on Homeland Security and Governmental Affairs, "Federal Regulation: A Review of Legislative Proposals, Part II," July 20, 2011, available at http://hsgac.senate.gov/public/index.cfm?FuseAction= Hearings.Hearing&Hearing_ID=6b0123b5-c6b2-42f2-9bfa-1b588af931d4. See also Sally Katzen, "Expand Centralized Regulatory Review to Independent Agencies," August 9, 2011, available at http://www.law.upenn.edu/blogs/regblog/2011/08/expand-centralized-regulatory-review-to-independent-agencies.html.

[107] Sally Katzen has suggested that the rules could be submitted to GAO or the Congressional Budget Office. See Sally Katzen, "Expand Centralized Regulatory Review to Independent Agencies," August 9, 2011, available at http://www.law.upenn.edu/blogs/regblog/2011/08/ expand-centralized-regulatory-review-to-independent-agencies.html.

[108] Other options include GAO or the Congressional Budget Office, although those agencies would likely require additional resources to take on this responsibility.

[109] See 44 U.S.C. §3507(f).

[110] Testimony of Susan E. Dudley before the Senate Committee on Homeland Security and Governmental Affairs, "Federal Regulation: A Review of Legislative Proposals, Part II," July 20, 2011, available at http://www.hsgac.senate.gov/hearings/federal-regulation-a-review-of-legislative-proposals-part-ii, pp. 16-17.

[111] Testimony of Peter L. Strauss before the Subcommittee on Courts, Commercial and Administrative Law, House Committee on the Judiciary, "The APA at 65 – Is Reform Needed to Create Jobs, Promote Economic Growth, and Reduce Costs?," February 28, 2011, available at pdf http://judiciary.house.gov/index.cfm/2011/2/hearing-on-the-apaat-65-is-reform-needed-to-create-jobs-promote-economic-growth-and-reduce-costs-0.

[112] Sally Katzen, "Why Congress Should Not Codify Cost-Benefit Analysis Requirements," July 7, 2011, available at http://www.law.upenn.edu/blogs/regblog/2011/06/why-congress-should-not-codify-requirements-for-economicanalysis-of-new-regulations.html.

[113] The scope of any such amendment would likely need to be confined to confined to Executive Order 12866 to avoid affecting other statutes and executive orders that reference the statutory definition of an independent regulatory agency.

[114] *Whitman v. American Trucking Associations*, 531 U.S. 457 (2001).

[115] *Entergy Corp. v. Riverkeeper, Inc.*, 556 U.S. 208 (2009).

[116] See, for example, Arthur Levitt, Jr., “Don’t Gut the S.E.C.,” *New York Times*, August 7, 2011, p. A19, who noted that when he was chairman of the SEC, the data needed to do a cost-benefit analysis was only available from large auditing firms, who would not provide the data. See also U.S. Government Accounting Office, *Federal Water Requirements: Challenges to Estimating the Cost Impact on Local Communities,* GAO-06-151R (December 1, 2005), which reported that local communities often lack the institutional knowledge or historical records on treatment technologies and, as a result, may not be able to provide cost information.

[117] A 1997 study by the Congressional Budget Office concluded that the median cost of 85 analyses conducted between 1990 and 1996 was $270,000, but some of the analyses cost more than $1 million. See Congressional Budget Office, *Regulatory Impact Analysis: Costs at Selected Agencies and Implications for the Legislative Process*, March 1997, available at http://www.cbo.gov/ftpdocs/40xx/doc4015/1997doc04-Entire.pdf. See also U.S. General Accounting Office, *EPA’s Costs of Preparing Regulatory Impact Analyses,* GAO/RCED-97-15R (December 6, 1996), which reported that 27 EPA analyses cost about $13 million, or an average of about $480,000 each. The cost of the individual studies ranged from $46,000 to $3.8 million.

[118] After the July 22, 2011, decision regarding the SEC’s proxy access rule, the Committee on Capital Markets Regulation (described on its website as an independent and nonpartisan 501(c)(3) research organization dedicated to improving the regulation of U.S. capital markets) released a statement saying, in part, that the SEC and other commissions “will not be able to do the necessary cost-benefit analysis without adequate funding,” and went on to say that “we support such funding.” See http://www.capmktsreg.org/pdfs/ 2011.07.27%20Proxy%20Access%20statement.pdf.

INDEX

A

B

C

D

E

F

G

H

I

J

L

M

N

O

P

Q

R

S

T

U